SHANNON:

WHAT'S IT ALL MEAN?

101 Commentaries by
wayne shannon

FIRST PRINTING, January 1987

Library of Congress Catalog Card Number 86-062501
International Standard Book Number 0-932916-13-9

Library of Congress Cataloging-in-Publication Data

Shannon, Wayne. 1948 -
SHANNON: What's It All Mean?

Includes index
1. United States—Social life and customs—
1971-   . 2. United States—Social life and customs—
1971-   —Anecdotes, facetiae, satire, etc. I. Title.
E169.02.S457 1986   973.92   86-62501
ISBN 0-932916-13-9

MAY-MURDOCK PUBLICATIONS
Drawer 1346 - 90 Glenwood Avenue
Ross, California 94957

Printed in the United States of America

꩜ ꩜

ACKNOWLEDGMENTS

A special thanks to "See Dick and Jayne" Murdock, of May-Murdock Publications, for having the courage of my convictions, to Mike Pechner who, as the saying goes, "started it all," to Warren Hinckle, of the *San Francisco Examiner,* for agreeing to do the foreword of "Das Book," to the kind folks here at KRON who hired me (most of whom were canned soon after), to Dick Van Wie, also of Channel 4, a long-time friend in deed, to Gene Wike and Don Brice, mentors, may they rest in peace, "Zoon"of KIRO-TV in Seattle (don't ask), Tom Snyder and Merv Griffin, Jim Harriott of KOMO-TV, Seattle, who gave me my first major on-air job, and Larry Sturholm, KIRO-TV, Seattle, who has pretty much made me regret it ever since. Thank you all.

W.S.

FOREWORD

"Hi, guy," the fat man said.

We were at Capurro's, a bar at the Wharf in San Francisco. I was there pouring drinks into men off the boats, looking for clues to the drowning at sea of three fishermen by a hit-and-run tanker. Shannon was there to drag me to an awful daytime TV program which was in its last throes on Channel 4, perhaps because the producers insisted on filming it in shopping centers which have to be among God's least desirable locations.

This particular center was in Hayward, or some such far away place. Shannon, dressed in a sweater that fit him like hoops on a barrel, had a driver in tow who'd parked a godawful yellow Rolls limo in front. It looked out of place, even among the garish tourist-trap signs blighting the Wharf.

The driver was a persistent little man in a chauffeur's cap who had the mannerisms of a British nanny.

"We have to leave right now," he said, "to make the show." I said the hell with the show, I was going to have a drink.

"No, we're leaving now," the driver insisted.

That was how the fight started.

Shannon had a friend with him, Pat Nolan, owner of the Dover Club, an Irish bar that has a clientele of gardeners, garbagemen, shipyard workers, pensioneers and drinking women. Nolan thought it hilarious that some "limey guy in a cap" would try to whisk us away from the bar, and ordered another drink.

The chauffeur-nanny nagged on, repeatedly going to the telephone to report us to the studio the way a person with a bladder condition goes to the bathroom.

Shannon, a peace-loving Irishman, was by this time trying to smooth things over.—"maybe we should get going, guys" —but Nolan, a man of the IRA breed, would have none of it. "Let's just have another wee little drink," Nolan said, setting up three more Jack Daniels and Cokes in front of Shannon. (If you ever wondered why he acts like that on the tube, now you know; a man is what he drinks.)

Finally, we were in the yellow Rolls Royce, racing down old

Nimitz freeway toward the dreaded shopping center to meet the tube-monster. Shannon was sitting up front, attempting to calm the driver. Nolan, the bartender, was in the back seat mixing Bloody Marys, which he had fortuitously brought along.

He kept trying to pass drinks over to Shannon (who declined since he had Jack Daniels and Cokes bubbling out his nose). And each time, Nolan spilled a bit down the neck of the limey driver who reacted by simultaneously speeding up and changing lanes.

The shopping center was covered with a great ugly haze, the color of day-old gauze on a wound. It was hot. The yellow limo screeched to a stop. The driver, florid-faced, ran around and opened the door to evict Nolan and myself, then followed us, with the certain lope of an assassin, through a giant back door into the bowels of the buildings.

Shannon and I sat on high stools amid hot lights in the awful humidity of the lower level of the shopping center and were interviewed by two professionally cheery types. It was, on the whole, a hideous scene unhelped by the mugginess.

But somehow through all this Shannon retained the good humor of a volunteer Santa. He even rode back to the city with the yellow submarine driver to cool the man out, although I would have considered drowning a better way to relieve the male nanny's anxieties.

When I called Shannon the next day to remonstrate against such a hellish situation, he said, "Hi, guy, wasn't that a great trip?"

Such is the unboundless measure of the man's optimism. He doesn't think anything is really bad, and even if it is, it's an object for humor, and that's good, isn't it?

In his mini-essays for TV, published in this book, one surprising thing is that Shannon who sounds smart when you hear him, also reads well in print. (If you think that isn't a unique accomplishment, try reading the transcript of one of Dwight Eisenhower's press conferences.)

Among my favorites is Shannon's commentary on the lack of servicing, according to a sex survey, of Brit wives by Brit hubbies. His conclusion is priceless.

When he is irreverent, which is usually, he's such a sly fox it sounds like he's being nice. Shannon is so smooth he could take the wrinkles out of a prune with a smile. He is one of those people who can fall into a mud hole and climb out with a fish in his pocket. Even the bad things that happen to him turn somehow good in his cheery spectrum; if he were eyeball to eyeball with God, Shannon would smile first.

He once told me that when he went to see the movie *The Right Stuff,* a man came up to him in the lobby and said, "You're the Chuck Yaeger of writers. You're probably going to die somehow from something you did stupid."

Shannon asked the fellow's name so he could put him on his Christmas card list. What can you say against a man so jolly?

Does he tell us anything about himself in these commentaries? He'd say no, but I say yes. Take the one in this book where he talks about his experience in junior high school English. The teacher told the class they could "cheat" on their weekly spelling tests, but only the five students who brought in the smallest "cheat sheets" with the 20 words written down could use them during the test. Darned if he didn't go for it, rewriting that thing each week until it was no bigger than a postage stamp!

Some people like him and some (surprise) hate him, and I must confess I've joined the former category even though every time I wander out into the world in his company I end up with at least a sprained toe.

But no one can dispute that Wayne Shannon is the genuine item. He is his own thing: He is not, as Whistler said of mauve, pink trying to be purple.

Warren Hinckle
San Francisco Examiner
September 18, 1986

DEDICATION

. . . to the ones I love; my children who were lost in the wars, my mother, LaYvonne, and the legendary Denise Paulette who could love among the ruins . . .

PREFACE

What follows are 101 of the essay/commentaries I wrote between July 1982 and the first part of 1986 while working at KRON-TV, Channel 4 in San Francisco, California. These particular ones were chosen either because of audience response at the time, or because they were recommended by friends and colleagues for inclusion, or because they were favorites of mine, in that order. I hope you enjoy them. Happy trails!

PS Not that anyone has ever asked, but my personal opinion of my career in television news, i.e. what part I played and what I consider my contribution, can best be summed up by the instructions for use of *Crest* toothpaste: "Squeeze the tube from the bottom and flatten it as you go up."

Wayne Shannon
San Francisco, California
January, 1987

TABLE OF CONTENTS

PART ONE

Humorous

LIFETIME WATCH

30 July 1982

This new wristwatch is a Swiss invention that will show up under the brand name of *Bulova*. It's called a "Thermatron" and, are you ready? It runs on body heat.

Yes, indeed. Which means, of course, if your son or daughter gets home one night and their watch is an hour fast, you'll know what they've been up to . . .

The Thermatron is due to hit the market in the next year or so and should cost about 500 magic beans. Specifically, it converts body heat into electricity that will fully charge the battery inside after only three months of wear. Once the battery is charged you can even take the watch off and it will still run for an entire year.

Now since the Thermatron runs on body heat, we've got a whole new definition for the phrase, "A Lifetime Guarantee." In other words, if you've been wearing that watch constantly and for a long time and then you notice that it has stopped, you have one of two *big* problems.

You've either got yourself a bad watch, or you've been dead at least a year.

S.F.O. HIGHRISE

5 November 1982

If you didn't know it, the San Francisco Bay Conservation and Development Commission has given the nod to Marriott Corporation to build a 100-foot tall hotel near the airport. Since it will be close to a particular runway, No. 19-L to be exact, airline pilots are saying, "Don't put it there because it would be hard to see during bad weather."

Pilots are funny that way. It seems the runway is used for occasional takeoffs and the pilot likes to "hang a left" at the end of that runway to avoid mountains. If the hotel goes up, planes will have to fly *between* the hotel and the mountains and much closer to the communities of Burlingame and Brisbane. And the airport *already* gets lawsuits from those two towns like you and I get heartburn, so the future should be fun.

Now the Marriott folks have compromised. They wanted the hotel higher than 100 feet, so they don't know what the hub-bub's all about and the commission agrees and points out that Runway 19-L is only used for one percent of all takeoffs from S.F.O.

However, that one percent happens when other runways are shut down during storms.

Are we getting the picture? You know, it's not that life is really stranger than fiction; it's just that fiction doesn't know what it's up against.

REAGAN'S RANCH HAND

3 January 1983

Fifty-eight thousand five hundred dollars a year for a Mr. Fix-It job? Why, I'd resurface a thousand miles of dental floss for that! And we're told this is just a part time position: The guy only shows up when the president is *at* the ranch, which is what, four or five times a year?

This ranch hand, we are told, is a former California State trooper and one-time chauffeur for Mr. Reagan while he was governor hereabouts, who now chops wood and clears shrubs, and we pick up the tab.

Well, there's only one conclusion to be drawn from all this; Mr. Reagan must have the nastiest set of shrubs in the universe. And for the fifty-eight-five you and I are paying the handyman, he'd better be the General Patton of shrub-cutters.

This Reagan ranch hand has an official title, don't you know, which is, "Associate Administrator for Policy Analysis and Development" in the U.S. Commerce Department's Telecommunications and Information Administration.

Which means he works for the C.I.A., right? Now if President Reagan is doing nothing more than employing an old and dear friend, fine, but if that's the case, then let's employ him with *his* money and *not* ours.

I think it was me who once said, "America can always use one more friend and one less federal employee."

HEART ATTACKS AND SEX

19 May 1983

This expert is the Chief of Psychiatry at Massachusetts General Hospital in Boston and the following is based on research that's soon to appear in a book he's written. Which with any luck at all will have pictures. (Sorry)

What the doctor is saying in essence is that sex and heart attack recovery can go hand in hand, unless you use a strange grip. (Not sorry)

And by that the doctor means heart attack victims who return to sexual activity with a partner of similar age can expect a better chance at full recovery. If, however, the doctor warns, one chooses to *dance* with an 18-year old decathalon champion, one better learn to drink wine out of a shot glass because there's no point in buying a whole bottle.

This theory on the effect of the age of one's partner, incidentally, is based on research done involving male heart attack victims in Japan. So the message the good doctor is giving us via Japan, then, is that sexual moderation is excellent for heart attack recovery but if you're not in to moderation, you're going to find out real quick where the Japanese got the word "sake."

SEX CHANGE

13 July 1983

It isn't the first time married folks have found a so-called skeleton in the nuptial closet, though if this Kentucky gentleman's wife was ever in the closet, she's not there now.

The reason for the lawsuit, of course, is that the wife had a sex change operation sometime before she married the fellow back in 1980 in Pasadena (ah, California!) and failed to tell hubby about the aforementioned "project transition." And you know you've got to be careful these days when it comes to the choosing of a mate.

As my sainted grandmother used to say, a rose by any other name could be Edward!

We are not told how hubby found out that his wife used to be one of the guys, but now that he does know, he wants an annulment and $10,000 for what he calls mental anguish. The ungrateful lout! And after she gave him the best years of her lives!

The annulment looks like a sure thing at this point and because the fact of the operation was withheld, we're talking fraud and who knows about the ten grand.

All of this reminds me of a travel poster I once saw in Amsterdam which read, "Not all marriages are made in heaven—some are fashioned in Sweden."

CHRISTINE'S CRAFT

9 August 1983

The first thing that has to be said is that Ms. Craft's accusation about TV stations altering a person's image is true to some extent.

I know it's most certainly a fact in my case. When I started this job a year ago, I was thin, had no grey hair and put my makeup on with a little tiny brush. Now I put it on with a trowel.

I'm in complete agreement: The beautiful people continue to dominate TV news and just because one has classic features doesn't mean that when the first tell-tale wrinkle appears we should be tossed out like an old pair of Gucci slippers.

I'll be the first to admit that, historically, the beautiful TV news personalities have changed my life . . . the flamboyant dresser, Ed Murrow . . . Andy Rooney's eyebrows . . . Charles Kuralt's Olympian thighs . . . Howard Cosell's naturally curly hair . . . and a name like Roger Mudd speaks for itself.

No, I'm sick and tired of being just another pretty face! And I now give public notice that I'm suing Channel 4 and the Chronicle Broadcasting Company, Inc. for $8.32 in punitive damages, while at the same time bringing suit to whichever firms consult Channel 4, for having the nerve to suggest that I am not "over the hill" physically, but in fact *am* a hill.

BIG FOOT HUNTING LICENSES

2 September 1983

A group out of Long Beach, California, calling itself "Sportsmen for Christ" has been turned down flat in an attempt to get a hunting license for, not one but two, "Big Foot" type creatures. The group wants a pair, we're told, for *scientific* reasons.

And whose job do you suppose it will be to hold the first one down while the other guys deal with the angry second one?

We have all heard of this mythological creature called Big Foot of course, though it is known elsewhere by many names such as "Sasquatch," "Yeti," "George," "The IRS" and "Haystack Calhoun." The difference with most of us being that we don't buy the existence of an 8-foot, bi-pedal beastie dressed in a designer shag carpet and neither, apparently, does the California Department of Fish and Game.

In fact, according to the D.F.G., even if the creature did exist— man, animal or vegetable—, they would hardly sanction open season on it and doubtless not for a group whose expertise in *Gargantua* might be suspect. Nope, if Mr. and Ms. Foot are out there, along with all the little "Bunyans," do let's allow them to live in peace and tranquility.

Actually, I only know one man who believed in Big Foot; my former football coach, "Lead" Reynolds.

But then what could you expect from a man who drank generic sterno?

LOVELESS BRITISH WIVES

13 September 1983

Well, I suppose we shouldn't be too surprised that three-quarters of the wives in Britain get little or no TLC from their spouses, if this British magazine survey is true. We colonials always did wonder how the sun finally set on the British Empire and now we know: Its men don't do well in the dark.

The sad or interesting part of this survey though, depending on your attitude, is that 3 out of 10 of the wives surveyed have acquired, how shall we say? . . . an extracurricular "Friend in Need."

And the reason for this, we are told, is that those wives find it easier to take a lover than to tell their husbands they are unhappy with the physical aspects of their marriage.

In other words, sports fans, since these women find it difficult to talk about sex with their hubbies, they go out and find a man of few words.

The survey also goes on to say that most of the 7,000 women contacted read *racey* books but care little for *blue* movies. It concludes that women prefer the use of imagination or fantasies to help heighten physical gratification and that a woman who is frustrated with her hubby but says nothing to him about it, is much more likely to be in the market for a Tarzan.

Now does this survey tell us much about British males? Most certainly. Just because they play a lot of cricket doesn't mean they've got a good grip or know how to swing.

BHAGWAN FOR ME

25 September 1983

You probably caught this story in the *Chronicle* article by Allyn Stone, but Swami Salam and many of his followers are packing up and leaving Berkeley for a communal ranch in Oregon.

The reason given, according to a spokesperson for the Bhagwan, as he's also called, is because he believes, quoting the story: "A catastrophe will level major population centers including San Francisco, Los Angeles, New York, Bombay and Tokyo." The spokeperson's name, incidentally, is Sunshine as in "You are my."

The Swami claims in the next 15 years California specifically is in for everything from natural to man-made catastrophes, which *he* won't be experiencing because he, his Rolls Royce and his Berkeley followers will be in Oregon.

We're also told that those who wish to follow Bhagwan into the north woods should do this as an act of love and ask no questions—questions like: "What is it that's going to wipe out California and do nothing to Oregon?"

I suspect an earthquake that moves from Los Angeles and then on up to San Francisco may not have the good sense to stop at Redding, and, if the good Bhagwan thinks Oregon can survive between Washington State's nuclear sub bases and the military targets from there to San Diego during WW-III, he'd better get himself another high gear in that Rolls Royce.

THE ELECTRIFIED GUITARIST

27 September 1983

What we have here is the lead guitarist for a group called the McDowell County Line Band, performing at a club called the Blarney Stone in Fountain Valley, a few miles southwest of Los Angeles.

It was not the Hollywood Bowl you understand, but the audience did get fired up when this lead guitarist took off on some spectacular "licks" as they are called, followed by some truly unique body gyrations, which was culminated by no less than a five foot leap, spinning and twisting through the air, out and onto the audience.

Well, for little or no cover charge you can imagine the crowd's response to a performance of that magnitude. In short, they were electrified.

And, in fact, so was the guitarist.

It seems somebody on stage tipped a beer over on this guy's amplifier, which sent "rockets" through the connecting wires to his guitar, through his body and mind and propelled him into a classic rendition of *Mama Don't Let Your Babies Grow Up to be Lightbulbs*.

Even with the voltage and the fall, we are told the guitarist is in good health and recuperating in his Huntington Beach home where he is doubtless considering a second career as a V.U. meter.

THE WORDMAN OF ALCATRAZ

10 November 1983

I guess I was in junior high, in English class, and at the end of each week we'd have a test in which we had to define 20 words and use them in a sentence. Obviously, a vocabulary test, and every week we got 20 new words. As each week passed, a lot of our grades sank like rocks because most of us were terrible spellers and hated homework. (Haven't students changed remarkably over the years?)

Anyway, about the fourth week into the school year the teacher announced that in the future, we could *cheat* on the weekly spelling tests. This is a true story. She said the five students who brought in the smallest cheat sheets with all 20 words written down and at least a one word definition, could use them during the tests.

Each week the five winning cheat sheets were measured by her, allowed to be used and magnifying glasses were okay. This concept was a large hit. I, for one, spent hours writing and rewriting that thing until it was no bigger than a postage stamp, using a magnifying glass and an architect's pencil.

Me and about six or eight other dummies got regularly high grades in vocabulary after that, never realizing that the idea we were getting away with something illegal had only raised our concentration a thousand fold.

And I've been known as The Wordman of Alcatraz ever since.

ACCURATE CONGRESSIONAL RECORDS
20 January 1984

As you may know, the daily Congressional Record is a written version of what supposedly happens on the floor of the U.S. House and Senate. An 1895 federal law says there's supposed to be a record so there is. But the problem, according to some, is that this written record is a long way from accurate.

Why is that?

Well, we are told our congressmen and women have a habit of tossing in items "for the record"that were never a part of the day's proceedings.

Like what?

Oh, letters from the home state on everything from birthday announcements to citizen opinions on issues being debated in Congress. It always wows the folks back home to read their names in the Congressional Record. And, after a bill has been passed, our elected officials have been known to even toss in a written speech or argument to make the candidate look a little better, or to imply they were on the floor longer than two minutes.

Some people hate this practice in Congress and a lawyer from Denver representing the *Mountain States Legal Foundation* wants it changed. What a "maroon" this guy is! He thinks our Congress is going to give up a boondoggle like that?

Not in this lifetime. Why a bogus Congressional Record is as American as an unbalanced federal budget.

My sainted grandmother was right, you know. Politicians are like rocking chairs; they're only level when you're sittin' on 'em.

SNAKE IN CAN

25 January 1984

I for one, continue to agree with Indiana Jones from *The Raiders of the Lost Ark*. Why is it always snakes? Right up there with spiders, cockroaches and earwigs, I hate snakes. And the larger the snake, the more fillings I lose when my mouth snaps open.

As everyone knows, the python is the Haystack Calhoun of snakes and this poor woman in West Hollywood found one today in her porcelain sit-down: Sixty-seven inches long and 8 to 10 inches around!

I can't speak for you, of course, but if that ever happened to me it would be English chamber pots 'til death do us part. Now when she saw this thing, curled up like a mile of kielbasa, she called two plumbers to remove it. And to say they refused to touch it is to say that Quentin Kopp has a way with words.

Eventually the woman called in the fire department which used carbon dioxide, forceps and a noose to get it out, the fire department speculating later that the python had slithered up the plumbing from the sewer, where it doubtless lived on a diet of let's not talk about it.

I don't need to hear that California sewers are an agreeable habitat for pythons—I mean really! I have never liked surprises in the bathroom. Since no one warned me there was such a product, it once took me three days to recover from the first time I saw that bowl full of *blue* water.

SHUTTLE TOILETS

10 February 1984

Here, sports fans, is what you call your delicate topic, so if you want to go to the refrigerator, I'll understand.

Actually, it's not *that* bad. But it seems on all 10 shuttle missions so far every crew has complained about, how shall we say, the non-gravitational, high-tech, intergalactic chamber pot.

In a phrase, it *don't* work right, and this, apparently, is a cause for consternation among our astronauts—no kidding! It seems to me, and it's pretty obvious our astronauts agree, that if you're going to spend "byll-yuns" on a space shuttle program and then expect these people to be up there any time at all, it is not too much to ask that the *conveniences* remain convenient.

The two satellites the crew just launched that misfired cost 150 million, the robot arm that won't, another 100 mil, and the balloon that popped, 450 thousand. In short, *money* can't be the problem.

This is no Winnebago up there; it's supposed to be the Lincoln Town Car of Buck Rogersville. And for that kind of money you'd think somebody could come up with a $38 plumbing job our astronauts could live with.

No, as my sainted grandmother used to say, "You can always take a horse to water, but be on your toes after that."

CHINESE NEW YEAR

17 February 1984

I remember well the first time I ever went to Chinatown in San Francisco to see the New Year's Parade. One of my elementary school chums was Chinese and my parents let me go with his folks to see it. This was when my family lived on Turk Street, near where Channel 4 and a freeway on ramp are now.

I was about nine years old and what was particularly nice about seeing the parade that first time was that my friend's parents lived right in Chinatown and had a fantastic view of said parade from their balcony.

But, as I recall, the balcony was awfully close to the ground and when the dragon headed our way and opened his huge mouth, a four-year supply of firecrackers went off! I guess my eyes got as big as hub-caps and I clearly telegraphed belief that this dragon was going to devour me in one bite. That was the same day I found out *tinkle* is also a Chinese word.

I mean, I *knew* the dragon wasn't real. As it approached I could see the legs and feet of the dancers underneath. But it's hard to be "cool" when you're eyeball-to-eyeball with a dragon of any description and at nine years old, "cool" is everything.

Well, the house of my friend's parents was packed with people and this scene, complete with my damp pants, caused roaring laughter.

However, I learned a lesson I have never forgotten: If you're going to see a dragon at work or play, watch your imagination, because imagination is "mother's milk" to a dragon.

HIGH-TECH KITTY LITTER

16 March 1984

High-tech kitty litter, it kind of assaults the senses, doesn't it? I suppose with all the innovation going on in Silicon Valley, we shouldn't be too surprised that deep thinking has popped up in Oakland also, even if, in this case, it appears to be something "the cat dragged in."

What we have here, Airwick fans, is the result of experimentation and two and a half years of market research in six U.S. cities with a product called *Fresh Step.*

According to the Clorox folks, the manufacturers, *Fresh Step* is the newest and best thing for your kitty's litter box because of its "micro-encapsulated mint-herbal scent" which is released into the air when your puddy-tat simply steps on the uh . . . product. It is "pressure activated" we are told and can't we all relate to that?

We are assured this advance in kitty litterdom is a definite improvement over the last genre breakthrough, which lest we forget, is a *moisture* activated product.

What's it all mean?

It means in the future if you're up in the dark, going for a late night "gargle" and the room suddenly bursts into a botanical garden, don't reach for the light. It's way too late.

SUPER BOOK THIEF

21 March 1984

I was about eight years old and the girl next door (we were play-ing inside because it was raining) breathlessly pulled her long skirt up above her knees. She did this to show me a series of small warts that went around each of her kneecaps like halos. She told me this was the "Dewey Decimal System."

I don't remember if I believed her at the time, but I've felt at home in libraries ever since.

Now, what's neat about a guy who has just been busted in Cleve-land is he claimed to have a strange attachment to libraries, also, when he was apprehended with several books, wrapped up in a newspaper, he hadn't bothered to check out.

He acted so strange, in fact, police got a warrant to search his home. And his house—virtually every square inch of it, waist deep—was covered with books, some of which had been missing from the neighborhood library for nearly twenty years, and were valued at approximately fifty thousand dollars!

When the police asked him why he stole the books, his re-sponse was simply, "I never got a library card."

I did get a library card, of course, several in my time. I figured I'd read until I got warts.

A HORSE IS NOT A CAR

23 April 1984

I don't know about you, but I didn't think the "is it a horse or a car?" debate was still unsettled. I remember once my Uncle Denzel was accused of confusing his horse with his Ford coupe because he said they produced the same product. But then, again, he's the only man in the history of the state of Idaho who ever successfully started a horse with a key.

What we have here, fans of the quirt and spurs, is a fellow in Louisiana who has been arrested twice for drunkeness while riding a horse. The official charge was "drunken driving" both times.

The second time he was caught he was in a horse/car accident, after which the horse had to be shot. That time a judge ruled the man had to pay $350 in fines and spend a month in the "barn."

So what does Red Ryder's lawyer do but take the case to a federal appeals court, pleading that you can't convict our hero of "drunk driving" because one does not *drive* a horse, a horse is not a vehicle.

And sho-nuf, the higher court agreed since Louisiana's vehicular code does not include animals, the court adding, "It is within the authority of the legislature, not this court, to enact such a policy."

So there you have it. If you must drink, don't drive. And if you must drive drunk, drive a horse. Anywhere but in Alaska; that's where my Uncle Denzel lives.

OLD CALIFORNIA LAWS

9 May 1984

The folks we are talking about here are in the State Assembly's Criminal Law and Public Safety Committee which has voted five to nothing to send a bill to the floor which, if passed, would eliminate a few laws on the books that are somewhat behind the times.

One to be tossed out is the 1872 law that says you can't sell alcohol within a mile of a religious revival meeting. Another is the one that carries a $1,000 fine and six months in jail for spitting in public. Another is a 1873 law which bans the exhibiting of a "deformity for hire." I'm gonna miss that one.

Another law to be axed is one that carries a $1,000 fine for the unsolicited delivery of razor blades. That should make cocaine users snort!

Then there's the 1913 law making it a misdemeanor crime to hide one's identity with a mask or false whiskers.

And last but not least, the California law which carries a $5,000 fine for seducing a virgin with a promise of marriage. According to the committee, the last complaint filed under *that* one was in 1923.

And we thought the California Condor was an endangered species!

"I KILLED WAYNE SHANNON"

28 May 1984

The San Francisco police called me at home at 6:30 this morning to find out if I was alive.

I don't know if it's still there on the sidewalk at this hour, in front of Channel 4, but somebody took some orange day-glo paint and a cardboard stencil and sprayed the words: "I killed Wayne Shannon." It was right out front here so the cops were called in and they started wondering if the statement was true and phoned me.

At 6:30 in the morning I felt like saying, "No, at this hour I'm quite dead," but eventually I figured it wasn't a put-on and I told the officer I was fine.

This, of course, left me with the mystical question of who would want to spray "I killed Wayne Shannon" on a sidewalk in *any* color paint? I had to immediately rule out the Ku Klux Klan, angry politicians and a couple of lawyers I know. None of them can write.

This left only two viable alternatives: Either a San Francisco comic or my mother.

And Mom, if it was you, it's not funny. I'm sorry your Mother's Day card arrived late. It happens.

STAR TREK III

1 June 1984

Star Trek III opened today in the Bay Area. A moment of silence please. Just kidding.

Of course, we "Trekkies" don't really know if (gasp!) Mr. Spock will be returning to life, what with his being bumped off and all in the last episode. We are simply to believe that one of *Star Trek's* most important serial characters is gone, never to be heard from again.

Surely they jest! It goes without saying that he will come back to life again, as sure as he has pointed ears and green blood and as sure as my Uncle Denzel performed the first *Vulcan Mind Link* with a quart of T-Bird.

If it happens you are not a Trekkie so have no idea what I'm saying and could care less about Mr. Spock and his body, now lying somewhere locked in a smooth black plastic coffin, which looks like something you'd store your vacuum cleaner in, with no soul since he loaned *that* to Bones, who doesn't even know he has it because he's been taking too many "hits" on that 300-year-old Romulan ale snuck through the neutral zone . . . then you don't know what you're missing!

And that's sad, because it also means when you hear the phrase, "Beam me up, Scottie," you'd only think it's something kinky involving a two-by-four.

THE PERPETUAL BURGLAR

8 June 1984

As far as I can tell, being a casual observer, your average "Class L" (as in Low Life) criminal mind has at least two basic design flaws. One, it thinks it's intelligent and two, it thinks everybody else is stupid.

Either one of those philosophies would guarantee failure for the vast majority of criminals. Together they have to be the greatest one-two punch since Thelma Ritter and Zazu Pitts.

So what we have here is a 30-year-old fellow from Chicago busted for burglary and hauled into court. He pleads innocent but the cops know better—so much so that from the day they arrested him and he got out on bail, they've had him tailed.

It turns out that after this particular court session, the thief's lawyer takes him aside and tells him what his fee is going to be, about a grand. The thief says, "No problem," and promptly goes out, the cops right behind him, and burglarizes a home. When they nab him he has about $15,000 in stolen jewelry.

His excuse? "I had to do it for my lawyer."

This means, of course, that Issac Newton was wrong when he said, "Everything that goes up, comes down."

What he meant to say was, "If enough keeps goin' down, you're goin' up, dummy."

THE PORCELAIN PRISONER

13 June 1984

I've always wondered what happened if you squeezed the *Charmin* too hard or too long! What we have here fans of the phrase, "Sanitized for Your Protection," is a man from Chalmette, Louisiana, who was visiting the city where "Hot dang!" begins every sentence, Nashville, Tennessee.

Our man from Chalmette rented a room in the beautiful downtown Nashville Hyatt Regency and almost immediately, by accident, locked himself in that special room where functional technology meets nature face to face.

All this apparently happened in July of last year and it's only now the fellow has filed suit against Hyatt. According to reports, "Houdini" pounded on the bathroom door and hollered for help, on and off, for four hours until a maid finally showed up to change the bed.

We are further told this was four hours too late. The fellow now wants 750 thousand big ones for psychiatric fees, lost wages and his "impaired ability to function in society."

If this guy is a genuine claustrophobic, he's doubtless had a bad time, but 750 grand is a bit much, especially for not functioning well in society.

If I were Hyatt, I *might* be inclined to pick up the tab on the psychiatric fees, but only if he could prove he can no longer function in a bathroom.

U.S. ABSTRACTS

26 June 1984

You may have heard about this, but what it is, is a compilation of facts gleaned from the U.S. Census data we get every ten years as well as from other sources at the national level.

This abstract, then, is pretty harmless stuff, no names, but kind of fascinating if you're into statistics or national trends. By looking for certain things, for instance, we find out that Nevada has the most crimes of any state and Mississippi has the most people on welfare.

New Hampshire has the most automobiles per one thousand people, New York state the fewest, which makes sense. When car insurance is 15 bucks an hour, who can afford wheels?

Massachusettes has the most doctors and Idaho the least (potatoes are nature's "whisk"). More Californians live near cities, Vermont is the most rural.

The federal government owns 89 percent of the land in Alaska and zero point three percent of Connecticut. Well, what's in Connecticut?

Wyoming pays the most for energy and Rhode Island the least. The most people earning 50 thousand dollars a year or more live in Alaska and the state with the highest birth rate by far is Utah. Good old Utah.

Now do all these statistics mean we are living in the wrong state and should move?

Nah, you wait and see. Somebody will leave New Hampshire to get away from cars, move to Utah and get run over by kids.

JOAN V. LIZ

29 June 1984

I feel inclined to say that when Liz Taylor is looking good, few look better.

But over the years as with some folks (cough), urban sprawl sets in. And it is perhaps unfortunate that in Ms. Taylor's case, comedienne Joan Rivers jumped on the bandwagon and made light of a very heavy subject.

But lo, this is a new day and on the set of a television network program entitled *Hotel,* who should show up but Elizabeth Taylor with a shock of blonde hair and minus many, many pounds.

When Joan Rivers heard about this new Liz look she remarked, "Another year of fat and I could have paid off the mortgage."

It seems Liz has spent recent months at the Betty Ford Center for Chemical Dependency in Palm Springs and while there, lost the equivalent weight of a Volkswagon Rabbit.

In short, which Liz is, reports are she is looking splendid and her spirits are high. My Auntie Daisy will not be pleased when she learns that Liz no longer looks like an overstuffed sofa. All her life Daisy wanted to look like Liz Taylor, and for awhile there, she did.

TWO-DAY TATTOO DELAY

3 July 1984

I can't imagine why some Americans believe that California owns the deed to "Loonies" or their "Tunes."

A case in point: The commissioners in Camden County, Georgia. Right off, we know that anybody who would name anything after Camden, New Jersey, is not chopping wood with the business end of the axe, right?

I mean, we're talking about an area where the founding father might well have been a butter churn. So, with that in mind, what we have is a Camden county commissioner who was in the Navy once and though he won't go into detail, came out sporting two tattoos on his leg—one of a pig, the other a banty rooster. Musta been one hell of a night.

Anyway, what does "Admiral Nelson" do now but have an ordinance passed to support his theory that if he had been forced *by law* to wait at least two days for a tattoo back when he was a swabbie, he would not be wearing the ones he has today—an ordinance that even when passed received major guffaws from local owners of tattoo parlors.

But how important is this new law really? It's a biggy because in that same county it's a one hour wait to get married and no delay at all to buy a gun.

In other words, in Camden County, Georgia, you can make the mistake of your life in one hour and blow your brains out two minutes later, but the tattoo that says, "This End Up" has to wait.

HE'S GOT A TICKET TO RIDE

7 July 1984

It's been pretty well documented by now that the job of police officer is a thankless one and has a lot to do with people who've been caught doing something wrong. On that *happy* occasion when it's you who have erred, it is incredibly difficult to believe your tax dollars have paid for somebody in a highly visible uniform to slowly walk over to you and say nice and loud, "You shouldn't have done that."

And I don't know whose idea it was to have the man or woman in that uniform sport the face of an 18-year-old.

Be that as it may, police officers can make a mistake that doesn't get them a lot of laughs either. For instance, a Ventura, California cop pulled a Volkswagon over the other day and gave who he thought was the driver a speeding ticket. The recipient was so nervous at the time he was speechless but eventually showed up in court with a picture of the interior of the Volkswagon. It was built for British drivers, so the steering wheel was on the right side of the van, not the left.

The cop had ticketed the passenger, not the driver.

I think it was Julius Ceasar who, when told Hannibal was coming over the Alps riding not horses but elephants, said, "What?"

MOON LANDING ANNIVERSARY

21 JULY 1984

I guess everybody remembers where they were and what they were doing when the major events of history occurred and I'm no different.

When the Eagle landed in July 1969, I was watching TV like everybody else. It was, after all, the late 1960's . . . I was young and confused, afraid of the future, had no money in my pockets, wore ill-fitting clothes, had a garish silver chain around my neck and my head was shaved: I'd just been drafted!

Stationed at the Fort Lewis Induction Center near Seattle, Washington, I remember thinking, "Oh-mah-Gawd, how I'd like to be on the moon with my man Neil." There I stood in the recreation hall, watching the one black and white TV set and seeing the moon dust fly away when the Eagle landed.

All of us applauded and cheered mightily. It would obviously be just a few moments until Neil Armstrong appeared and hit the infield. But before that happened, what did I see out of the corner of my eye, through an open door, but a drill sergeant headed our direction holding a clip-board.

I'd only been in the army two days, but already I knew instinctively the Sarge was looking for "volunteers." I shot out a far door not unlike a spit-wad (I was thinner then), escaped mess duty but didn't see Neil Armstrong's epic walk, "til many moons later on a news program in Vietnam . . .

From where, as you may have surmised, I never returned. I'm Burt Parks.

WENDY NELDER FLUORIDATES AIDS

5 September 1984

Wendy, I have to be honest with you: This is not the best way to become mayor someday and for two reasons.

One, because the name "Wendy-don't-drink-the-water-Nelder" won't fit easily on a campaign button, and two, if you have to try and link AIDS, which showed up in town in 1978, to fluoridated water, which showed up in 1952, don't, for crying out loud, throw in cancer, premature aging, arthritis, bone disease and hunchbacks.

See, if you go that far, you wind up on the side of people who believe that fluoridated water is a Communist plot to destroy America. These people are loons, Wendy, arrows with no feathers.

Every politician has a few loons in the constituency, we all know that, and they are the first ones to point out that fluoride in concentrated form is used to kill rats but that's not a ball you should pick up and run with, Wendy.

You put 500 pounds of dried milk in a sack and drop it from ten feet, that kills rats, too.

Now, Wendy, be assured, we know your heart is in the right place but give us a break! You are never going to tie hunchbacks and toothpaste together in this lifetime.

JOHN HINCKLEY JR. WANTS TO VOTE

6 September 1984

Like a lot of Americans, I continue to this day to be flabber-gasted at the Hinckley verdict of "Not Guilty" and it'll be a cold day in Thermal, California, before I change my mind.

He shot the president, which we all saw on national television. He should, therefore, have been found guilty, judged to be *crazy,* and put in a rubber room in Washington D.C. (where he is now, though not rubberized) Then, slowly and carefully, he should have been nurtured back to squeaky-clean mental health, shown a video tape of what he did when he was a *Looney Tune,* and, after that thrown right back in the slammer.

But since he's just a boy "with problems" and not guilty of any-thing, he feels he now has a right to vote in his home state of Colo-rado. And while he's at it, he's also asking for phone and unscreened mail privileges and an opportunity to hold a press conference whenever he wants one.

Colorado authorities are saying that since Hinckley is not regis-tered to vote there, he won't be allowed to do so, *this* fall anyway. And thank heavens. That would have been, literally, delivering "soup to nuts."

So John Hinckley Jr. wants to vote, does he? You know what we ought to do with ole John, don't you? We ought to have him flown out here to San Francisco . . . and have Wendy Nelder give him a *big* glass of water.

THE NIGHT THE LIGHTS WENT OUT ON NADER

10 September 1984

Maybe I've mentioned this before but I worked in Detroit a few years back as a consumer reporter. One of the more humorous moments I recall from those days was when a Chrysler PR man asked me if I "am now, or ever have been, Ralph Nader?"

Nader is not a popular man in Mo-Town, not because he doesn't have a right to do what he does, but because so much of it appeared on the front pages of newspapers and thereby helped to undermine American confidence in the U.S. auto industry.

But then, a "one industry" town is funny that way. If you want to get a real big laugh in Detroit, just drive past a U.A.W. picket line in a Toyota.

Well, anyway, the subject here is voters and specifically when Ralph Nader addressed the 200 or so who came to hear him at the Unity by the Sea Church in Santa Monica. Nader told the minister that his speech would be for the sole purpose of convincing people they should register to vote, a noble goal, certainly.

So later, the minister is sitting there next to the podium, when Nader starts taking pot-shots at President Reagan. The minister gets up, kills the mike and the lights, and calls the meeting to a close.

He said later he would have done the same thing had Nader bad-mouthed Mr. Mondale. Nader had simply over-stepped the bounds of his agreement with the minister and got The Hook.

It's one of the reasons religion and politics should never mix: Not enough politicians believe in hell.

COCA COLA JEANS

11 September 1984

MurJani, the company that makes *Gloria Vanderbuilt* jeans has just bought the rights to make *Coca Cola* jeans. Good heavens!

I have to be honest with you. Though I am quite used to seeing *Coca Cola* in cans, I am not prepared to see "cans," in *Coca Colas.* In fact, I for one will never wear anything on my body that is based solely on a product that makes me burp.

Next, we have the obvious zipper controversy. I don't believe that strongly in aluminum and I don't even want to think about a series of pull-tabs. I'm telling you this entire concept is fraught with bizarre possibilities. First comes *Coca Cola* jeans and then before you're aware, somebody's trying to recycle your underwear.

And if *Coca Cola* can do this, why not *General Motors,* or worse yet, *Wham-O?*

I mean, think about it. How'd you like the phrase *Land Rover* or *Silly Putty* emblazened on your bumper, so to speak? And what about the candy manufacturers? How are you ever going to get a date wearing a pair of jeans that say *Snickers?*

Nope, I believe corporate logo clothing is a questionable idea, especially when it comes to carbonated soft drinks. Do you realize that a diet *Coke* may someday be a snide remark about a pair of short-shorts?

TWO THIEVES TWO

18 September 1984

The first story we're talking about here is a meat market owner in Florida who, for the past two years, has been selling veal to his customers for about half the normal price.

A good buy, obviously, so he had a lot of takers, though over that two years he also had a good number of complaints from consumers.

Well, the Florida Department of Agriculture ran a little test the other day on the veal this turkey was selling and that's just what it was—turkey! There was no veal at all. He's now facing a $5,000 fine and up to five years in the icebox.

Next, we've got the story of a regular visitor to the municipal zoo in Houston, Texas, who, over a period of nine months, noticed the coral snake in one exhibit never moved an inch.

The guy contacts a local newspaper and tells his story, the paper checks it out only to have zoo officials say, sure, it doesn't move because it's rubber. When asked why, they said it's because real coral snakes die every four months or so in captivity and you don't have that problem with the rubber ones.

What's interesting is you can bet those people running the zoo don't think of themselves as being in the same league with that clown and his zero percent veal but they're exactly the same.

And that's what makes thieves interesting in general—some don't know they're in the business.

SCHOOL SEX PAMPHLETS

21 September 1984

Has public school changed or what? I don't know about you but when I was going, there weren't any pamphlets on sex. I grew up thinking that "procreation" was a union of fundamentalist clergy. And I don't care how many biology classes they gave me, I was well into my senior year of high school before I knew for sure I had something in common with frogs other than warts. What possible use could I have had for sex education? I had zits and put Jade East on with a turkey baster.

But be that as it may, now we have the California Office of Family Planning cranking out two pamphlets, paid for with part of a ten million dollar state grant, to be used by teachers as "aids" to teach students "sexual awareness."

A couple of topics for discussion in these pamphlets include "Sex is like food; it is more enjoyable when you have variety," and "How important is virginity in this day and age?" They also mention the pros and cons of contraceptives and abortion.

As you might imagine, some parents and/or taxpayers are not too happy with these pamphlets, but what makes the resulting lawsuit a bit more intriguing is that it may open the door to challenge state funded abortions. So stay tuned . . .

All of this, of course, has arrived much too late for me. I mean, the way things turned out after school, I could have easily given up sex for Lent.

ORGAN DONOR CHARACTERISTICS

1 October 1984

There's a medical opinion in the October issue of the magazine *Psychology Today* that comes to us from a psychiatrist at the University of Illinois Medical School. What he's saying essentially is: You need a heart, I kick the bucket, you get my heart and my heartburn. Or you *think* you've got my heartburn . . . You follow that?

In other words, according to this doctor, there are two theories about how people can react to organ transplants. First of all, the recipient can have a psychological reaction to the new organ based upon who the person was, or is, who donated the organ.

The doctor says if the recipient thinks they got a kidney from a nice person, the recipient can become nicer. Conversely, should the recipient believe they got their new kidney from a creep or a chump, they go to the bathroom more often. (That last is just a guess.)

Now, the second possible reaction, according to this doctor, is the body's basic response to an alien organ—that something's not quite right—which the doctor says is akin to an adolescent imbalance when a person's natural organs are not maturing at the same rate. And haven't we all been there?

That's the latest news on organ transplants: They may lead to transplanted emotions as well. And if you'd like to know more about this phenomenon, see the Mel Brooks' film *Young Frankenstein*.

101-YEAR OLD GROOM

5 October 1984

Okay, fans of the book *The Sun Also Rises,* we have here 101-year old Arthur "Yumpin'-Yimminie" Jonsson, a well-to-do farmer and horse dealer who lives about 110 miles southwest of Stockholm in the little village of Askersund. (I tossed in that "Yumpin'-Yimminie" part myself; that's not really his nick-name. It will be but it's not at the moment) . . .

Now, Jonsson has been a bachelor all of his 101 years and though his health is excellent, he decided recently to hire a permanent nurse to attend him, a live-in nurse that is, because, as the Swedish like to say, "Ya yoost never know."

So in comes a nurse who later tells the newspapers she was only planning to stay two weeks until Yumpin' could find full-time help. She adds though that in those scant two weeks, she and this incredibly old and rich farmer began to fall madly in love.

According to newspaper reports, 55-year old Ingrid Engdal and 101-year old Jonsson announced their engagement at a ceremony attended by her four grown children from other marriages.

What's it all mean?

Well, it means that my Aunt Muriel was right: Never fight a ball of yarn. Just be patient and it'll fall in your lap.

THE MAYFLOWER MADAM

17 October 1984

Yes, I realize this is a tacky subject but it's my job to let you know when "things are changing" and, friends, they are. We're talking about an estimated one million dollar a year operation with 28 "operatives" numbering among them actresses, models and dancers.

The clientele included Arab sheiks and corporate officers from all over the world. An hour of—how shall we say?—*consolation,* ran as high as $400, with a full evening flat rate of 12-hundred beans, not including gratuities.

The entire operation was run from a westside Manhattan townhouse where records, both excellent and voluminous, were found. They included who paid what, when and how, as well as proof that the 28 *employees* had one of the best group health insurance plans available.

The 32-year old woman who is the purported owner and manager of this little home for wayward executives is an Ivy League college graduate who majored in, and rightly so, *business management.* "Let Me Call You Madam" is now out on 75-hundred dollar bail but before she left her precinct cell, she hung a makeshift diploma on the wall which named her "Woman Executive of the Year."

A million dollar a year business up in smoke. And what, dare we ponder, will this do to the index we lovingly refer to as The Gross National Product?

THE '84 DOUBLE-SPEAK AWARDS

16 November 1984

George Orwell, as you may remember, wrote the book *1984* which projected a world controlled by "Big Brother" and included an official government language he called "Double-Speak," meaning to hide the truth.

What we have now, then, is the National Council of Teachers of English holding its annual convention in Detroit and handing out what teachers call their "1984 Double-Speak Awards" for misuses of language with more potential to cause harm than garden variety jargon and gobbledegook. (They're talking about *me* in that last part.)

First place this year went to the U.S. State Department for officially replacing the word "killing" in future documents with the phrase, "unlawful or arbitrary deprivation of life."

Second went to Vice-President George Bush for misquoting Democratic presidential hopeful Walter Mondale on a comparison between liberals and Nicaraguan leftists.

Third place went to our own Caspar Weinberger, U.S. Secretary of Defense, when he said of the removal of American troops from Lebanon, "Nothing has changed, we are not leaving Lebanon."

Other phrases that received awards included the invasion of Grenada, described as "pre-dawn vertical insertion" and last but not least, the National Transportation Board's description of an airplane crash as "controlled flights into terrain."

If you ask me, kids, it all sounds like we're headed up an unsanitary tributary without means of locomotion.

THE WEE BANDIT

27 November 1984

Here we have, fans of crime and punishment, a 22-year-old man who walks into a bank in Oxnard (I ask you) and gives the teller a note saying, essentially, put the money in the bag, I have a gun even though you can't see it.

Like most intelligent people, the teller thinks, what the hey, it's not my money and puts some 13-grand in large bills in the guy's bag while hitting the silent alarm. He does observe that "Al Capone" is incredibly antsie, but attributes that to problems doubtless inherent in the guy's line of work.

Our crook grabs the bag with the big bills and he's out the door on foot, quick like a bunny. Now, unbeknownst to him somebody from the bank decides to follow his escape, which ends up at a coin-operated laundromat not two blocks away.

Once inside, the thief starts taking money out of the bag, frantically looking for, we finally figure out, a small bill like a fiver or a dollar so he can use one of the laundromat's coin changers.

Why? Because it seems our man "Capone" has to do what little crystal bells do, *tinkle*. The bathrooms in the laundromat are coin operated, don't you know, and he has no change. So he can't *go* anywhere!

All this to be followed quickly by the arrival of Der Polizei as we learn once again that time and tide wait for no one.

THE EXOTIC OBJECT
1 January 1985

As I understand it, when one tries to peer into space over great distances so many stars get in the way you essentially end up staring at a *Handy Wipe*. And that's where this telescope in Hawaii comes in.

Its infa-red *whitchit* gets rid of a lot of extra light around the stars and you can see farther. That in mind, these astronomers and scientists aimed the telescope at the center of the Milky Way and found, in simple language, a *belly button*. And to hear them tell, there's a ring of hydrogen around it. Which makes me hope it *is* a belly button and not something else.

In technical terms, they're calling this thing out there, as mentioned earlier, an "exotic object." That's not too technical, but it's a phrase that certainly stirs the imagination. I mean, we could be talking about anything from a galactic keyhole to a shoehorn, though concensus is it's probably a great spinning star of immense size or even a black hole, as they're called.

A black hole, as you may remember, has a gravitational pull so outrageous that even light cannot escape its grasp. (We have something like it here on earth, but it's called divorce court.)

So there you have it. Experts say the Milky Way may have a navel so to speak, which if true, of course, makes our little planet lint.

SOVIETS SHOOT FINLAND

2 January 1985

You see, this is why I don't bother with diets anymore. There isn't going to *be* a year 2000.

I mean, let's face it, we have Pershing II missiles falling off trucks on I-5 not that they could do anything anyway, and now we have a little testing going on at sea by the Soviets with what amounts to a cruise missile (no armed warhead, happily) and what does it do when launched but land 200 miles off course in the wrong direction from whence it was aimed, mind you, augering in some two miles from a resort lake in Finnish Lapland.

Typical of Soviet austerity, the thing had no muffler so it rattled windows the whole way leaving the Norwegian government fit to be tied.

And if you haven't been reading the European funnies lately, Norway, prior to this event, was hardly a fan of, how shall we say, the Big Red One. You remember the Soviet submarine that got stuck in the mud off some fiord awhile back and the Norwegians tried to sink it with depth charges?

Well, Moscow hasn't had a Christmas card from that end of the world in a decade, and '85 is looking dim already.

You know what we need, don't you? We need some Idaho dirt farmers and some five-year plan folks from Soviet Georgia in high government positions on both sides. Simple people. The ones who have long known that if you only have *one* milk cow, you don't eat it.

BACK-PACK NUKES

4 January 1985

Why is it I'm always the last one to hear about stuff like this? NBC news just aired a program on back-pack nukes, as they're nick-named, mentioning that we not only have hundreds of them here and in Europe, we've had them since 1963!

I'd just discovered *Clearasil* in '63, what was I doing? The idea is this little nuke weighs in at about 60 pounds, we drop it and a commando behind enemy lines during a war, the nuke gets put in an appropriate place, the commando sneaks off and, using a remote control device, hits the button marked "gangbusters" and that's it.

The blast, by the way, is equivalent to the power of 250 tons of TNT plus radiation. Hand-held nukes? Mother of Pearl, wait until the toy manufacturers get a hold of that franchise.

The only friend GI Joe is going to need in the future is a detonator. You know, the military fact that never ceases to frighten me is the one that says an American nuclear submarine is the sixth most powerful nation on earth.

And now we have a disgruntled, underpaid staff sergeant stomping through a forest with the power to wipe out Leningrad? Of course, we should take some consolation in the fact we've had these things for decades. The Russians couldn't possibly have their own version.

Kids, don't put off "Club Med" another day. Get those shorts on and get out in that ocean while there are still some fish in it!

NEW SHUTTLE TOILET

11 February 1985

In the movie *A Summer Place,* I remember there was a big storm swirling and battering this island hotel and Beulah Bondi came downstairs to complain that there was a leak in the roof. She tells Dorothy McGuire about it, whereupon Richard Egan volunteers to fix it, which leads to Dorothy and Richard going upstairs together alone which leads to a rather torrid wet shirt and spit-curl scene in the attic, which leads to a clandestine meeting later in a boathouse, all of which gave us the phrase, "I'd rather be sailing."

Now why do I mention this? Because that leak—the one Beulah Bondi mentioned—was in Beulah's bathroom and dripping directly into the center of what Beulah called "one of my conveniences."

I have never forgotten that line and it's the very same convenience that's been giving our astronauts fits in space and which NASA tells us has now been solved.

It cost 12 million dollars to develop, with a per unit purchase price of one million. And I guess there's no way to say this but to say it. What they've come up with is, essentially, a vacuum cleaner in which the astronaut's body completes the circuit. No body, no vacuum, and after two shuttle flights now, it works like a charm with the end result being jettisoned into space.

Boy, let's hope we *are* the only planet with life as we know it: If we've got neighbors this is going to strain the relationship.

BURIALS IN SPACE

12 February 1985

A story came out in the newspapers awhile back that a company in Houston, Texas, *Space Services, Inc.,* wanted to send human ashes into the cosmos. I thought I'd let it pass to see if the government would go for it, and go for it they did.

Next comes the testing of Space Service's small rocket, we're told, and if that checks out, the phrase "this end up" is going to have a whole new meaning.

If you're interested and have the money, (about four grand) here's how it will work. First, you kick the bucket. You then get cremated, not once but twice. This isn't just neatness, it's so your remains can fit easily into a little capsule about half the size of a can of *Beenie Weenies.*

Then you, and ten thousand and 29 other ashes, are placed in the nose cone of a rocket called a "Conestoga" (from Oregon Trail fame). This rocket, we are further informed, will be launched from either Vandenburg Air Force Base here in California, or from a NASA facility on Wallops Island in Virginia. (I vote for Wallops.)

Then it's up, nineteen hundred miles in orbit, in a container that will glow in the dark of space so it can be seen from earth for the next sixty-three million years.

Am I going up? Yes, but not by way of a "Cones . . . toga" party. A fellow in Berkeley assures me that, for a nominal fee, I can go up alone, as soon as he finishes something he calls a "Laser Spit Wad."

DI FI AND HINCKLE

15 February 1985

I've been getting a lot of calls lately about two stories in the local news. One, the Warren Hinckle "crime wave," and the other, Mayor Dianne Feinstein's somewhat surprising statement about what a good idea it would be to build a dome over Candlestick Park. After about the tenth call, I got the feeling I'd turned into a radio request program. But there are a couple of reasons why I've left these two stories alone.

The "Free Hinckle" movement for instance: I thought it was doing fine without me. And I'd already done a commentary about Mayor Di Fi's burning desire to build a new sports stadium in downtown San Francisco, south of Market, maybe.

Remember, I said she'd never be able to convince my mother a new stadium could cost less than it would to put a top on Candlestick, so I'd keep my mother out of town?

Well, none of that mattered to the people who've called recently.

So . . . as for Warren Hinckle, that bastion of common sense, even in the face (or worse) of "The Great Marilyn Chambers Now-Defunct porn Bust," I tip my hat. As for his arrest on charges of a cavalier approach to animal leash laws and the like, "Legs" Hinckle will live forever in my mind as a man who knows that crime not only pays, it creates meaningful work for others.

As for Mayor Di and this brainstorm about a domed Candlestick, Bravo! I only wish I'd thought of it.

AMERICANS DON'T HAVE FUN BOOK

21 February 1985

There's a new book called *Leisure in Your Life: An Exploration* by a professor at Pennsylvania State University in the Parks and Recreation Division. We didn't have a parks and Recreation Division at the college I attended. I think the closest we had was a wood rasp and a ball of yarn, but that's another story.

According to this Penn State professor, though, you and I don't know how to function in a leisurely fashion anymore. The reason for that, he says, is our approach to work.

In other words, we have become so organized, so competitive, so goal and success oriented that fun and work are the same.

"We gotta be in Yosemite by 9am, Ethel. Move it!" . . . that sort of thing. I mean, how many people do you know who have turned the morning jog into the Boston Marathon, a picnic into military maneuvers and made bouncing balls seem like a racquet?

This professor tells us with certainty we are simply not a fun oriented society because even our leisure time activities are just another "nine to five" in terms of pressure, deadlines and competition.

Now me, I don't have that problem. I haven't accomplished a thing since the Vietnam War . . . and there are even those who claim we lost that one.

MOON THE RUSSIAN DAY

28 March 1985

I don't have to explain to you what "mooning" is, right? You are, hopefully, aware of the fact that over the years the word "moon" has made the nearly impossible transition from noun to verb. Grandmother liked to call verbs "action words" and "moon" is now most definitely an *action* word. I, for one, am glad Grandmother didn't live to see the moon make this transformation, though, as often happened, I might again be severely underestimating her ability to "go with the flow" of modern life.

Anyway, what we have here is an FM radio station in Long Branch, New Jersey, that has been promoting a "Moon the Russians Day" to commence at 6pm tonight on a beach set aside for nude bathing. Those who are bent on doing so may bare their emotions in the general direction of the Russian mainland. This, a protest for the recent death of an American soldier in East Germany, will include various and sundry other complaints against the Russian tendency to be trigger-happy and paranoid.

I trust the television networks, maybe even NBC, will cover this event so that we can all bare witness to yet another moon seen around the world.

Now, if you still don't know what the phrase "to moon" means, I would show you but for two or three reasons. One, you're not ready for it. Two, you're not Russian, except for those over on Green Street. And three, a TV license is hard to get back once you've lost it.

THE BOOTH THAT JOHN BUILT

4 April 1985

What we have here is the Maryland State Senate with an ocean of bills it passes in a flurry on the last day before the spring recess. And one of the bills in this stack of goodies, which were all passed by unanimous voice vote, was tagged *Tudor Hall.*

That bill, we are told, calls to set aside $50,000 to qualify for Federal matching funds, all of which will be used to restore a so-called "historic dwelling."

So *Tudor Hall,* and a whole mess of other stuff, flies through the Senate, everybody goes back to the office, grabs their gear and heads home, except for one Republican senator, who starts leafing through the bills he just helped pass. And that's when he notices the small print in the Tudor Hall bill that says this historical dwelling is the ancestoral home of the man who shot president Abraham Lincoln, John Wilkes Booth.

This does not amuse the senator who says to himself, "Wait a minute, 50-grand in Maryland taxpayer's money and another 50-grand belonging to Mr. and Ms. America, is going to be used to bring the home of John Wilkes Booth up to code?"

Not if *this* senator can help it and he decides to go to the media with the story, which makes the proposers of the bill crawl under a hail of rocks, and since the Maryland House of Representatives has yet to vote on *Tudor Hall,* it looks like it was caught in time.

What's it all mean? Vote. It can make a difference.

BANGKOK VASECTOMY

22 May 1985

I want you to know up front that I thought for a long time before I decided to use the word "vasectomy" in a commentary. Obviously because you never know who's listening, and if one of the persons listening with you is young enough, you're going to get stuck with the question, "Gee, Mom or Dad, what's that word mean?"

And you're going to have to say something like, "Well, it means that idiot up on the screen is going to be out of work in about two minutes!" Though I can't worry about that, I've got lawyers to support.

But whatever the word, that's what this guy in Bangkok is getting and what makes this story interesting is his *seven* wives have been trying to get him to agree to this operation for many moons. Word is that he agreed to do it only if it does not adversely affect his sex life.

Even though so-called "minor" wives are allowed in Thailand, this fellow is quite famous there. Now our problem with a story like this is we just can't imagine anybody being *that* interested in sex, but it's out there kids.

I remember once I heard a phrase in Asia that freely translated means, "I want you so much a hand comes out of my throat!"

TIMOTHY LEARY SOFTWARE

27 May 1985

Does this melt your butter or what? And looking back, we should have seen it coming. I mean, where else did we think righteous indignation of the 1960's was going to end up if not for sale in a shopping mall 20 years later?

What we have seen so far: Huey Newton and his cookbook, Eldridge Clever fashions, to be followed now by none other than the one-time advocate of "rolled and pleated" grey matter, Timothy Leary, out to sell a home computer game that can only be purchased by those who didn't follow his advice to begin with.

"Tune in, drop out." Remember? Boy, I missed that phrase *clean* the first time. I thought he was talking about a bottle of *Lydia Pinkham*. But be that as it isn't, according to our former fearless leader, this new home computer game will cost about 40 bucks, if we're so inclined, and is based on his own theory of "psycho-Geometry" which he tells us allows people to measure human behavior just like atomic particles can be measured. Right.

Different programming titles in his upcoming game includes "Social Sophistication," "Personal Dynamics" and "Life Adventure."

And, of course, if anybody's life has been an adventure, it's ole Tim Leary's. There are few among us, I figure, who owes as much to gravity as he does.

FUNGUS THAT EATS TOXIC WASTE

13 June 1985

It seems there's a theory going around that says providence supplied humanity with all it needs to solve its problems right here in earth. (You have to say "providence" now-a-days lest those who worship tinted glass demand equal time.)

I mention this theory because you never know, it might be true and if it turns out that a tree fungus can solve our toxic waste problems, we've got one big vote in favor of the aforementioned theory.

We are told that some researchers at Michigan State University, in cahoots with the U.S. Environmental Protection Agency, started looking into a fungus that rots dead trees, a fungus specifically called "white rot." Though I always thought white rot was a racial slur from Columbia in reference to cocaine. Anyway, your American lab heavies have been curious about this fungus for years ever since they found out it dissolves, or makes harmless, a chemical in wood called "Lignin," which also happens to be the toughest chemical in wood.

The theory eventually developed, then, if this fungus can eat anything that tough, how about trying it on toxic chemical wastes, and guess what? It eats everything from DDT to Polychlorinated *Be-Pee-Nals,* whatever they are.

All this information and more is coming out in the June 21st issue of *Science* magazine. I keep that one right next to my comic books. So there you have it. Maybe no more burning or burial of toxic chemicals because they've found a tree fungus that eats 'em.

I guess the next step will be to find out how much money the research eats.

SEX IN SPACE

24 June 1985

If you have heard of, or are familiar with, the so-called Mile High Club, that's essentially what we're talking about here. If, on the other hand, you have not heard of the Mile High Club and don't know what it is, that's *still* what we're talking about.

It seems there's this federally funded research group which has been given the task of recommending to NASA what it thinks a future space station should contain to make astronauts comfy and happy during a sustained stint in space.

It has come to light through an article due out in the July issue of *Psychology Today* that this very same research group has recommended to NASA—just a thought really—that NASA's space station *might* contain sleeping quarters, how shall we say, with room for not just one but *dua*.

To quote the article, "If we lock people up for 90-day periods, we must plan for the possibility of intimate behavior." Now that's what I call a giant step for mankind. Plans for construction, we are told, would include either sleeping quarters large enough to accomodate the "hoo-hah" ramification outright, or there could be two sleeping areas separated by a partition that could be removed.

The research group says they don't want to over emphasize this possibility in space, but that NASA must take it into consideration. What's it all mean? Two things. One, NASA really does think of everything, and two, I believe this puts gravity in perspective, don'ut?

LEAP SECOND DAY

30 June 1985

I don't know what bothers me more, that somebody actually made an effort to find out a miserable lousy *second* needs to be added to the clock because the earth is slowing down, or that somebody who did that thinks you and I care.

I mean, what kind of a mind would worry about something like that? We have more nuclear warheads in the world today than Hitler's entire family had skin pores, we have cancer, bad water, bad air, bad cheese, bad luck, and for lack of a better word, we've got the *Shiites* in Lebanon.

I have this picture in my mind of these people at the U.S. Naval Observatory in Washington D.C. pouring over computer readouts when all of a sudden one of their faces go ashen, he or she squints, double checks the figures, walks over to a big table in the middle of the room, slaps the printout down hard, which causes the others to come over and look. Whereupon they all shake their heads in disbelief. The project leader says, "There's no chance for error. It's *got* to happen tonight. We're short an entire *second!*"

Gimme a break! I am a big fan of high technology. It's infinitely better for us than not, but this atomic clock thing has grown people running around looking for a lost second.

The I.R.S. is right, you know: If you don't see it, you don't miss it.

S.F. FAST-FOOD FREEZE

24 July 1985

As you might imagine, this story first popped into my mind when grown people in the Broadway area, long considered by most of us to be the garden spot of San Francisco anyway, got up in arms at the idea that a Carl's Jr. Restaurant was about to besmudge the escutcheon of North Beach.

In other words, the good citizens along and near Broadway, with its blinking neon nipples and signs that promote everything from "Oh-My-Goodness" to "You've-Got-to-be-Kidding," can't take the cultural clash of a fast-food store?

And now we're told that our city fathers (and doubtless a few mothers) are considering a city-wide fast-food freeze lest the *gold* of San Francisco turn into one big McNugget.

Come on, folks, lighten up! What do you think you're doing?

There's nothing intrinsically wrong with a fast-food restaurant, with the possible exception of the food. But they are businesses, and businesses, most of them, that are packed to the rafters with customers. They pay every kind of tax there is and are one of the few places on earth these days where young (and even some old) people can get a job.

Ninety percent of the owners of these restaurants are even willing to have them blend into the architecture of the surrounding buildings and are not trying in infiltrate residential areas. They're like me; they don't want to butt in where they're not wanted. But you city supervisors should approach fast-food stores, or anything like them, on an individual or neighborhood basis. And if you go with a city-wide freeze, you're nuts. Trust me, I'd know.

RUSSIAN SUB TRACKS IN THE SEA OF JAPAN

29 July 1985

I'll be perfectly frank with you. I'm not over the arrival of killer bees in Bakersfield yet. And by that I mean I don't think it's too much to ask that I be given a week or two between major surprises. I was just getting used to the fact that some state-of-the-art *bug* could attack and kill my car and now we hear that the Russians not only have submarines like little tractors that run on treads but also, they've been down there so long and been so busy they have everything but traffic lights!

Japanese intelligence gatherers say these submarine tracks on the bottom of the Sea of Japan, six different sets, were first spotted sometime last year. And I guess the only reason we're hearing about it now is because of a *Time* magazine interview coming out, given by a Japanese defense official.

What happened to *Star Wars?* I thought *up* was the only direction we had to worry about. I don't want little red *Tonka Toys* coming out of Carquinez Straights.

You know what this means, don't you?

That's right. We're not only going to have to catch those killer bees in Bakersfield, we're gonna have to teach them suckers to swim.

SNAKE BITES PREACHER

19 August 1985

Before you get on the phone and complain that I'm poking fun at either religion or death, don't. I'm poking fun at *idiots,* and that's different. It's not my fault that some idiots have a connection to a particular religion or that they die.

So we have this preacher out in Tennessee who uses poisonous snakes in his sermons and it turns out, as in most states, there's a law in Tennessee that says nobody, no how, can use dangerous animals like poisonous snakes in religious ceremonies.

The preacher did it anyway and a local sheriff showed up one night, tried to get the snake away from the preacher and got bit by the snake, and the sheriff spent eight days in the hospital recovering. The preacher gets arrested and fined. End of story? Not quite.

A few days later, with another snake at another sermon, the preacher tells his followers the reason that sheriff got so ill, was because he was a non-believer in the Bible which makes mention of handling of serpents.

However, during this second sermon, the preacher himself gets bitten. He holds a prayer vigil for a miracle cure and within 36 hours, ta-da, he's dead like a rock.

You know, that's probably the biggest drawback with your wackos. Every now and then, they're in charge.

ANCIENT TEETH

27 August 1985

Maybe it's me, but I'm getting a little tired of various and sundry "experts" telling us that just about everybody who lived before us had it better than we do. I mean, I'm even starting to feel we're better off with The Bomb because for the first time in history a world war is *completely* insane versus *basically* insane.

And now we have this report from some guy in Scotland who says that by studying human teeth from the Stone Age we may assume that those who lived then had fewer cavities than we do now, by far, specifically stating that 4.1 percent of the ancients had tooth decay as opposed to 90 percent today.

Well, hell's afire, that's no mystery. Back when hens really had teeth, there weren't any *Twinkies, Cheerios or Miracle Whip,* none of life's essentials. And besides, the old timers had fewer teeth to begin with and all the while without fork one, having to be able to field strip a pterodactyl or whatever. I mean, can you imagine the kind of *uppers* those people must have had to be able to eat raw meat on the run because something chasing them had the same thing in mind?

Nah, this Scot's blowing wind up our skirts. Sure, cavemen had fewer cavities, but there's a reason for that. You don't have bad teeth when your life expectancy is four minutes.

LABOR DAY

2 September 1985

I don't know about you but I never know what to *think* about Labor Day. The only thing I'm sure of is that my mother doesn't want to discuss it.

But other than that, what's supposed to come to mind?

We can, obviously, dwell on the American labor movement, i.e. unions, and can therefore recall the great strides we've made in terms of salaries, job security, pensions, health and other benefits the unions doubtless helped to bring about.

Or we can dwell on union dues, strikes, picket lines, lock outs and some union mucky-muck in New York donating a half-million of *our* dollars to the "Lithuanian Society for the Prevention of Cruelty to Tramp Steamers."

Or we can simply consider American labor in general, the products and services we Americans provide for each other. Everything from hamburgers to letters in our mail box. (Well, let's don't talk about the mail.)

And then there's even little ole me, giving you the kind of information you just can't get anywhere else which I like to call "News You Can Abuse."

Yes, I think the real message behind Labor Day is that we Americans are all dependent upon each other. The key to everything is *dependents*. At least that's what my ex-wife's lawyer tells me.

HUMPHREY THE WHALE

16 October 1985

What is with this whale? I mean, we've heard everything from it was scared into the bay by the Navy ships that showed up for Fleet Week to a guess that the whale may have an inner ear problem or infection that might have harmed its internal compass.

Well, we know one thing for sure. If it ends up going as far as Sacramento, it's definitely ill. Of course we can only hope Humphrey, as he's been nick-named, is a democrat. Fat democrats are always *suspected* of being dishonest, but with a fat republican you just *know* somehow.

Latest reports say Humphrey is now circling in a deep channel a few miles west of Sacto, after that round-about journey from San Francisco Bay up the delta, and uh, that certainly sounds like a democrat. One of several concerns though, is that the inland route Humphrey's taking is through water with considerably less salt content than the ocean, and that could be a serious hazard, specifically to Humphrey's eyes.

So with a bad compass to begin with, added to the potential of fuzzy vision, we're going to have to face a dire possibility.

Old Humphrey could easily become our next governor.

DOG AND CAT MOUTHWASH

18 October 1985

You know, when I first stumbled across this story about a dog and cat mouthwash, I said to myself, "Come on!" But after reading about it, hearing the manufacturer's justifications and the expected acceptance by American pet owners, I then said, "Come on!"

Has somebody got too much time on their hands or what? See, there's this big conference being held in Denver on Saturday and pet product manufacturers from all over the country are meeting and that's where this new mouthwash is going to be introduced.

It's a spray bottle. You hold your dog's or cat's mouth open, squirt a little Pooky on Rhubarb's front teeth. Then the animal goes nuts with its tongue, of course, and that we're told, serves to move the bacteria-killing spray and deodorizer throughout the mouth.

I remember once in San Anselmo on our back porch one night, I gave a *Milk Dud* to a raccoon. He musta rolled around out there for half an hour trying to get that thing out. And initially anyway, I would expect something similar from your pet, vis-a-vis this mouthwash.

No word yet on how much the new product will cost but as my sainted grandmother used to say, "Money is no object, when you're buying something you don't need."

WIVES WHO HIDE MONEY

22 October 1985

Before I started writing this story I checked with several married women in the newsroom here at Channel 4 and virtually all of the ones I talked to said they have money somewhere that their husbands don't know about.

One said she fudges with the checkbook. In other words, when she deposits her check from work, she writes in 200 bucks less in the register than she really deposits.

Still another has a joint account with her mother and periodically deposits money into that, all of which their husbands know nothing about.

One married guy overheard me talking and told me he knows of his wife's hidden money, but she doesn't know he knows, and he's not going to bring it up because *he's* got some money hidden somewhere, too.

Maybe it won't come as much of a surprise to some of you, but I feel like such a dummy. I didn't know this sort of thing was going on, did you? Anyway, the survey in *Working Woman* magazine says that one out of five wives who hide money does so for reasons that range from personal selfishness to a fear that someday they might be destitute following a divorce or the death of their hubby.

What's it all mean? Apparently it means some women don't just live longer than men, they *earn* it.

JOURNALISTS IN SPACE

24 October 1985

I ain't goin' and that's for the record. There's nothing in space I want and anything in space that wants me is just going to have to lump it because, like I say, I ain't goin'.

I pretty well had to give up the title of journalist when I took this job as a humorous essayist/commentator and now that NASA is offering to spend 80 grand turning a journalist into a long-haul dock worker, I couldn't have lost the title at a more opportune moment. I fully realize that NASA wouldn't be inclined to send a fat person up there anyway, but if you think I'd start exercising and eating wheat germ just so I could *moon* North America in one pass, you're nuts.

Not on a bet would I go up in one of those things. Half of what they take up there they don't come back with and two-thirds of what they do leave up there they've got to go back for later. And besides, they've gotten so democratic about who flies in the shuttle anymore there's no telling what you'd end up with.

Think about it: Eight to ten days and nights, no gravity, one clown and no exits. Nope, if the good lord had intended me to fly He would have put feathers all over my . . . well, certainly where they would have done the most good.

DIVORCE SHOWERS FOR MEN

20 November 1985

Now this is what I call the mountain coming to where Mohammed used to live. And it's a terrific idea. It seems a lawyer in Manhattan got a divorce some 18 months ago and with his former spouse went, if you couldn't guess, everything that wasn't nailed down except, of course, whatever he had in his pockets, which you can bet her lawyer got.

Anyway, some friends of this guy heard about his plight and decided, what the hey, how's about we throw him a divorce shower and replace some of the things he used to have. You know, silly things like silverware, plates, cups, glasses, a toaster, sheets, pillowcases, towels, a lamp, a chair maybe.

Forgive me. I get carried away. I used to own things once. But now there's another twist to this story which is, we are told, that Bloomingdale's and one or two other stores, are asking single people to register at the store, like a bride and groom might do, so in the event of birthday, or a divorce, somebody might buy you what you need or want. Is clever?

Does this new wrinkle called *divorce shower* say anything about the current state of our society?

Oh, yah. If you take too many showers, eventually you drown.

CABLE CAR RATE HIKE

20 November 1985

We have it on pretty good authority that 85 percent of the people who ride San Francisco's cable cars are tourists. That being the case, I say, "Do it," as it were. "Stick it to the tourists! Hike the rates."

I mean, think about it. Some of these people come from as far away as Australia, what are they gonna do when they get here after a trip like that? *Walk* up Powell Street?

Not on your tintype, mate. No, no, I say. Up the fare on the cable cars from one bean to two for three reasons. First, half the people who come to San Francisco do so just to laugh at us anyway, two, the other half visit to buy original art deco, and three, that added dollar would throw an estimated four point seven million extra hooties in the city's kitty, which could help lower Muni bus "fast pass" tickets, which us locals could use a lot.

Get the picture? We *got* tourists, they *got* tourists, we *got* cable cars, they don't. They wear Bay Rum, we wouldn't be caught dead in it. So if the tourists come here just to remind us rock and roll built this city and polyester built theirs, they can darn well pay one buck more, as they say back east, "to take a sit."

THE BIG GAME

22 November 1985

Here we are waiting for the 88th edition of the Big Game with heavy rains predicted again for the 411th year in a row as the Cal Bears and Stanford Cardinals go at it claw and feather, as it were.

Now, in the tradition of crack sports journalism, alá Howard Cossell, am I going to project the winner of this year's game? In a word, uh-uh. I have the tires on my car to consider. I figure if somebody got really huffy, they'd even puncture the spare and I'm just not ready to handle *five* flats.

Nope, to find who's going to win the Big Game tomorrow, we'll just have to wait like the footballers themselves. May the best team win and may the losers find solace in the fact they did so in front of a whole lot of people.

What's it all mean? Well, it means the game of life is like the game of football. It's a heck of a lot of work, it seems like it lasts forever but it's over before you know it, it's filled with many fumbles, the occasional pass, much pain and a myriad of penalties, the odd ball, some stitches.

And every now and then, usually when you least expect it, you'll get it in the end zone.

ANCIENT TOMB AIR

24 November 1985

For the life of me, I have yet to figure out why some people are so fascinated with ancient Egypt. I mean, so what if they developed everything from a chemical battery to the written word and could fit stones together with such precision that it matches the work of today's lasers. And all of this long before Julius Caesar got his first hickey.

Now NASA, the *National Geographic* folks and the Egyptian Antiquities Authority, just to name a few, are going to spend one-point-five million dollars to suck the air out of an old tomb they found a few years ago near the big pyramid in Giza. It doesn't take much to amuse some people, does it?

Anyway, we are told this old air, which will be extracted carefully by a system once used on Mars to test the Martian atmosphere, may prove useful in preserving what will later be uncovered in this tomb. You follow that? One-point-five million *drakmas* to reproduce the overall effect of my Aunt Muriel's attic?

I don't know, maybe it's just me, but tombs give me the heebie-jeebies. It has long been my opinion that still waters don't run deep, they run slimy.

MUSIC-OVER-SEX SURVEY

26 November 1985

When I first heard about this survey in *Psychology Today* where red-blooded Americans actually chose music over sex, I said to myself, "Whoa, get out the life rafts, we're sinking like stone." I mean, Wolfgang over whoopee? Handel over *hoohah?* Hewey Lewis and no News?

There had to be a foul-up somewhere. And sho-nuf, 'pon reading the details it turns out this survey was originally printed in another magazine five years ago, which means the data is old to begin with. Secondly, the people who were asked to list their thrills in order, who put sex in sixth place and music first, were, in fact, all *musicians.*

Does that make a bit of difference or what? Of course musicians are going to put music above sex. Ask anybody, four or five years in a band and only the trombone players remember *how.*

And where does this survey come from, mind you, but a professor of pharma-psychology at Stanford University, questioning students attending Stanford. Now who in their right mind is going to ask the Stanford band about anything? Especially sex! Two thirds of that bunch cost their school a football game a couple of years ago, and why? Because they didn't know one end from another!

Nupe, people treat surveys like bowling balls. They give them too much weight and they're full of holes.

FORTY-NINERS LOSE DIVISION TO RAMS

9 December 1985

Even the most died-in-the-wool 'Niner fans have to admit we were simply out-played in the division game. I think it was Ka-nute Rockney or some such type who once said of the game of football, "It's difficult to win *without* the ball!"

Since our boys in the red and gold made it their life's work to give the football away, obviously forgetting the Ka-nute's timeless observation that you can't win without the dang thing, the Los Angeles Rams played up to their potential. They didn't need to play up to their potential, of course, what with the Ka-nute's advice not being what you'd call an *intregal* part of the 'Niner huddle during the game.

But then, we don't want to imply for a moment that we here in the Bay Area are something other than good sports, even in the face of a losing effort by our heroes.

No. We do not want to leave that impression.

What do we want to leave the Ram football team and its loyal fans with? Oh, how's about Annie Oakley's little known but apt motto: "Eat . . . shoot . . . and die!"

CAROL DODA RETIRES?

21 December 1985

It never ceases to amaze me how much goes on right in my own backyard that I know nothing about and I'm in the news business. I mean, we *got* machines, we *got* journalists, we *got* computers, which we are told they *don't got*. You 'spose the KRON ad campaign was designed by an English grammar major, "We got, they got?" Somehow I doubt it. A multi-million dollar operation with a thousand years of college trained writers and we couldn't come up with a single "they've" got?

Oh well, what do I know? Carol Doda is giving serious thought to a life off center stage, and everybody tells me they've known about it for a couple of weeks now.

According to Ms. Doda, the club where she used to work wanted her to take a pay cut. Whereas, on the other hand, club management says her option, though doubtless much else, has been dropped.

Even though her live stage career in *public* may be coming to an end, Ms. Doda says that *private* performances may be in the offing as well as her participation in an exclusive phone conversation service. (cough)

What's my reaction to all this? Well, even though I have never seen Ms. Doda do her . . . how shall we say, "interpretive dancing", I have often looked upon her presence on San Francisco's great Broadway in the same light I have looked upon the bombers of the Strategic Air Command. It was good to know they were out there.

IS THERE A SANTA CLAUS?

24 December 1985

See, this isn't the easy job you always thought it was. I now have to go on record, in public, and state whether or not I, as in "me," actually believe in the world famous and dearly beloved Santa Claus.

We know, of course, that when one is a child it's okay to say "yes," while if one is an adult it is not fashionable to admit that this mythical character actually exists. I call him mythical because, I guarantee you, I've never *seen* him.

The next obvious question being: Am I stalling? The answer to which is: Yup. But let me, here and now, deal with the big question, which is really several questions.

Could there be a person who is virtually unselfish, who only gives and almost never receives? Yes, I think we've all known a few people like that . . .

Could there really be someone, somewhere, who, no matter how bad the weather, would travel a great distance just to see us? I should think so . . .

Might there be a person somewhere who is joyously alive and happy and whose very presence never fails to lighten our hearts? One or two, yes . . .

Finally, though, could only *one* person have all these qualities? Is there really then a Santa Claus?

Obviously, there is and furthermore I believe in my heart of hearts that whoever is Santa Claus must have wanted to be Santa more than anyone else did. Which means, little ones, if you wish with all your might, and never, ever give up trying, even you, someday, could be called by that wondrous name.

SHUTTLE COLUMBIA FLIGHT CANCELLED AGAIN

9 January 1986
(19 days before the shuttle Challenger exploded)

Don't get me wrong. I love the space program and I know the value of a reusable shuttle as opposed to the old days when we had to sit there and watch millions of dollars in rockets go into the Atlantic like so much Alka-Seltzer.

I'm not saying we want the old days back. What I am saying is, why are we trying to launch one of these things every 14 minutes? If that was me up there surrounded with a fortune in bathroom tile and they kept cancelling the flight, I would have a tendency to say, "My, how fun flies when we're having times, and this is one of them."

Come on, I can't be the only person who thinks NASA shouldn't feel obliged to match the departures and arrivals of the Greyhound Company, all right? Just take it easy, there's no rush. What's NASA hauling up there anyway but a couple of satellites and some unhatched eggs from Kentucky Fried Chicken? (You don't want to know.) And let us not forget the object of the space program: To get humans up, around and about, and back down again in the safest and most efficient manner.

Therefore, when we have a half-dozen cancellations of a particular flight, let us take pause and assume that fate may be trying to tell us the same thing my sainted grandmother once told me and I quote: "You gotta cold button somewhere?"

THE LOIS LANE SYNDROME

26 February 1986

If this idea of American women meeting with disappointment in their lives due to a shortage of real life supermen seems like a ideological rip-off of the earlier concept called "The Cinderella Syndrome" then you are not alone.

That's exactly what it sounds like to me also. But then we here at the old "Double-Duce" just report the news and let you draw your own conclusions, except for me of course. I fall all over myself giving you my conclusions which the vast majority of you have the good sense to ignore.

Be that as it may, Dr. Joyce Brothers says, according to her experience, there are three types of women who look in vain for the non-existent Superman. One group searches for such a fellow because it's tied to their image of themselves. If they strive for perfection, any potential mate must be perfect also, though Dr. Joyce says, surprisingly, women in this group, deep down inside, feel extremely inadequate.

The second group, she says, are afraid of close relationships altogether and therefore set *impossible* standards for a man, which means a close relationship is also impossible.

And finally, some women want a Superman-type to replace, how shall we say, daddy.

What's it all mean? Well, it means that if you must find a Superman you are certainly in the right town. Trust me, if there's anywhere a man can change in a phone booth, it's in San Francisco.

CORDLESS PHONES DIAL 911?

14 March 1986

You know what gets me about this? Who would have thought to look at the possibility a cordless phone, or *any* kind of phone for that matter, could dial anything without the help of a human being?

And how could you check out the bizarre theory (if you came up with it) that when batteries run low on a cordless phone, it'll pick up the vibes, as it were, given off by refrigerators and microwaves and pass them along the telephone line as the emergency digits, 911?

I'll tell you what, if there's *anything* that frosts my cookies more than having my phone calling Paramedics without my permission, it's having my kitchen appliances *force* my phone to do so in a weak moment! See, don't let anybody kid you, George Orwell is not dead. He works for an electronics conglomerate in Taiwan, all right? I mean, it wouldn't be your average Joe or Josephine, would it, who would think to put a nation-wide 911 emergency phone number on the same frequency as the motors that run a frost-free and a heatless *widget?*

Life is not on our side. Not when we've got Kelvinators talking to what's left of Ma Bell. No, no. First chance we get, we have to move back to the rural areas. I knew machines would take things over someday, but I never assumed they'd phone ahead for reservations!

PART TWO

Serious

THE JAPANESE INTERNMENT APOLOGY BILL

16 June 1983

My mother was a teller in a San Francisco bank for many years, and one of her dearest friends is a Japanese-American woman who was also a teller in that bank. It took a long time, but eventually the two women decided their husbands should meet for dinner at one of the two homes.

That dinner was held at the home of my mother's friend in the late 50's, early 60's, and I went along.

My father, a World War II Navy veteran, had fought in the Pacific and the husband of my mother's friend spent much of his youth in a U.S. internment camp. My mother's friend was actually born in such a camp. My father lost many friends and relatives in the war, and his opposite had had to watch his father die while interned.

You can, perhaps, imagine the tension that night. In short, the two men would never develop the friendship their women had, but when we moved from California a few years later, we all met one last time, at our house, I believe. That night the two men got drunk and, though the women pretty much left them alone, they were seen laughing together.

My point: All the misery, all the hatred aside, the internment of Japanese-Americans was a colossal mistake and those who have the sense to know it should indeed apologize. And just as important, that apology should be accepted.

Surely, from that point, we can best guarantee such a thing will never again happen to an American.

MARINES DIE IN BEIRUT

24 October 1983

Our dead will be coming home soon, as they have since any of us remember. We are told they are dead because these small controllable skirmishes are better than world wars, where millions are buried instead of thousands or hundreds.

I suppose they have a point but it will make no difference to the parents and loved ones of those Marines or those of the dead French soldiers.

Now that we don't have world wars any more, isn't it amazing how many die in the name of peace-keeping? What we continue to ponder, then, is how is it sane people can't keep from killing each other? The obvious answer being that everybody *isn't* sane when it comes to certain issues and beliefs.

To drive a truck filled with explosives through an iron gate and into a building on a suicide mission is a lot of things, but *sane* isn't one of them. The people behind the act say they want peace, too, but only on their terms. They don't want somebody to "dictate" a peace.

We're in Lebanon this time, word is, to tell the various warring factions, "If you fight each other you have to deal with us, so don't fight because we're bigger than all of you combined."

Not a bad theory, really—*if* everybody were sane.

THANKSGIVING

24 November 1983

You know, we're a strange lot, Americans. There isn't a race, creed, color or nationality on earth we don't number among us. We have more problems for that very reason than we can count and to top it all off, we have a document that says personal freedom is one of several truths we know to be self-evident.

We have hopes and aspirations that half the world doesn't even understand because they either can't read, or find survival the only thing they can afford to spend time considering. And the Eastern Block just plain doesn't think it can work because, according to them, personal freedom is just another phrase for decadence or chaos.

We're the free world's strongest nation and our allies are happy with that because it puts us up front so that our nose gets hit first every time. Those who despise us get around us by not playing by the rules, which means we have to play by *their* rules sometimes, which we hate, and which means they win even when they lose.

And God, the only name the American flag will bow to in honor, the Eastern Block rarely *officially* recognizes as existing. The question is then, just who do we think we are, and what is it we're thankful for?

We clash in personal lifestyles and philosophies and demand of our nation what none has ever achieved; real freedom for ourselves and for all who hunger for it. We've got to be nuts.

It is a sweet form of insanity, is it not? And I thank you for your frustrated part in it.

NANCY KULP FOR CONGRESS

31 January 1984

There's no point in my denying this. I love Nancy Kulp. She, without question, is one of the finest character actors in the history of the business, especially as a comedienne, and belongs in the glorious company of such talents as Thelma Ritter, Zazu Pitts and Una Merkel.

These women, and to a greater degree Nancy Kulp, had the splendid capability of taking "nothing" roles and transforming them into brilliant expressions of humanity, and almost always stealing the limelight and critical acclaim from the so-called "big name" stars they worked with.

In the 1955 through 1957 TV series, *Love That Rob,* Nancy played Pamela Livingston, a homely, skinny, flat-chested bird watcher who tried to compete for the attentions of Robert Cummings against classic looking female models who could often take or leave Bob.

In that role of the plain woman who never thought of herself as plain, Nancy became a national hit and would only solidify her image later in an even bigger show called *The Beverly Hillbillies*.

There's no telling what she would bring to Congress if elected, but if she shouldn't get there, Nancy Kulp has already supplied her nation with an invaluable service, a lesson. That lesson being: There are two kinds of beauty in this world, the skin deep variety, and the real thing.

Find out the difference, take what you were born with and run with it all the way to the top where Nancy Kulp lives—and belongs.

DAVID KENNEDY DIES

25 April 1984

There have been few families in the history of our nation who have played both a unique and a continuing role in national politics. American families who fall well within those guidelines are the Adams' who produced two presidents, the Roosevelts who did the same, and the Kennedys who, had fate been different, might have been the first to produce as many as three.

Of that select group though, the Kennedys were the greatest target for tragedy. What ghastly luck to have three sons die violent deaths and to have the 13-year-old son of one of those watch his father assassinated on live national television.

That father, of course, was Bobby Kennedy, and the son was David, who is now dead as well.

It's a long time before children can appreciate this, but no matter how tall they grow, no matter how intelligent and well educated they become, or how successful, or how old they get, their parents, especially their mothers, will always remember them best as babies, profoundly helpless and innocent.

So, if we are inclined to weep for Ethel Kennedy, it should not be for the loss of a son who is, or was, embroiled in drugs and possessed a damaged heart. That's not what she lost.

She lost her baby—which is much much worse.

MEMORIAL DAY

28 May 1984

If it so happens the thing you want to do for a living is to become a writer and one day you acquire that title, you're faced with a couple of problems. If you write humor, you will fail because humor is a matter of opinion, and when you write about serious matters, you must reach the heart of it all or you're no writer at all.

And when it comes to a topic like the day we set aside to honor Americans who have died in wars, the writer has an even greater obligation. Not so much to those who died, or even to veterans still alive, but to American children playing and picnicking on this day in parks, playgrounds, and backyards. The ones who, as yet, have no idea where they fit in terms of the world's hopes and dreams, no sense that they are the young and untried "royalty" of freedom.

We can argue whether our war dead fought in the right or in the wrong wars for the right reasons, but that we are here to argue at all we owe to those whom we honor today.

So, if the obligation of the writer on this day is to speak for those who can no longer speak because they gave all there was to give to children they would never see, I would say for them, to those children, "Play."

THE FOURTH OF JULY

4 July 1984

One could say, I guess, that you and I are 200 years old today. *Who* we are is certainly that old, though I for one don't feel my age. I feel young, way, way too young. Younger than China, than Rome, than Great Britain. I suspect we are growing older *faster* than any of those, however, since America's childhood was so short and the burdens we carry into the future are so ponderous.

Chief among those peculiar burdens, it seems to me, are American concepts, ideas. The lesson of Rome was clear: No one breaks away from a strong parent nation and comes out alive. A fact that remained true well into the 18th century. But America did it anyway, the first ever, and produced a Declaration of Independence, a Bill of Rights and a Consitiution that haunt us 200 years later; the most extraordinary documents in the world to date and, in combination, equal to the *Sword of Damascus* or *Excalibur* depending upon your viewpoint.

And oh, don't we Americans have differing viewpoints?

But 208 years later we're still here and dealing yet with the towering minds of Adams, Washington, Franklin and Jefferson. They and their partners in British treason, didn't ask you and me about any of this. They could doubtless only pray that if and when we came to be born, we would understand. And we do.

Happy birthday, kids.

CUOMO & JACKSON AT THE D.N.C.

17 July 1984

I'm assuming you've been watching the Democratic National Convention at home and heard Governor Mario Cuomo of New York speak last night, and then tonight, the Reverend Jesse Jackson. I was out in the crowd both times, and though admittedly much more often during Reverend Jackson's speech, people were actually crying.

What I found interesting about this is that those people on the floor are just like you and me. They've got a variety of opinions about Governor Cuomo and Reverend Jackson, though a good number of people didn't seem to know much about Cuomo.

But the point is, unknown or not, the audience was riveted by what these two eloquent and forceful Democrats had to say. And tonight Reverend Jackson did what he's famous for, aimed that enthusiasm and intense style directly at his audience. The ground shook with the stomping feet of those in the bleachers. I'm telling you it was terrific out there, and you know why?

Because, when Reverend Jackson hit those topics, touched the feelings that run through most Americans, found the notes to our common melody as it were, this place came right apart.

For the Republicans in Dallas, their opportunity to bring the best of their ranks to the microphone will come, too, and I wish them well. Because when it happens, when Americans gather together like this to fight for the future, I tell you the chills come down like diamonds from a shoe box.

VALENTINE'S DAY

14 February 1985

I don't know if you've ever heard this or not, but the idea is that every TV and radio signal or show ever done is still bouncing around the earth's atmosphere and, perhaps, even winging into unchartered space.

It's probably not true of course, and considering some of the essays I've written, hopefully not. But if it *is* true, I'd like this to be intercepted in the future—a Valentine's Day sonnet to my children.

As songs go, it was the best. It's borrowed
Solely for the purpose of this poem. . .
Got the rights to it in dreams. The music's
Mine because the lyricist said . . . sure . . .
The only words are in the title. Irritating,
Isn't it? The rest are matted
Into streams and dreams, the trust you make
Or take and break, the air you breathe, the trophies
You Receive . . . The song's inside a strand
of hair, regardless of your caring. It's in
The dirt, your food, your moods, above the truths
You claim, beneath the lies you blame. It's known
Before and as I'm leaving. He wrote it, and
Ages hence, it's called, "Your Father Loved You."

IWO JIMA ANNIVERSARY

19 February 1985

One hates to visit misery, to walk up to the door, knock and enter, but it must be done every now and again.

Forty years ago today, the U.S. Marines landed on an island in the Pacific, heavily garrisoned by the Japanese Army. And a battle began that lasted *five* weeks and took 29,800 lives, (we think; there were too many pieces to be sure).

One battle, one island, and on the fifth day, on a hilltop that could be seen from virtually every point on the island, an American flag was raised that would be immortalized in a photograph most Americans recognize to this day.

How ever did two nations, Japan and America, allow each other to produce a battle like Iwo Jima or any other battle for that matter? But we did and we are responsible for it.

It's easy to blame the leaders who failed us, who failed to find a way to resolve problems that were not worth the price we paid. The heroism and selfless sacrifice of those who fought and died on that island 40 years ago is beyond reproach. But also undeniable is the stupidity that put them there.

The world can no longer sit idly by and watch a Hitler come to power and then simply become a part of some dreadful snowball running down hill.

People are responsible for their leaders and leaders are responsible for the world and that's the lesson of an Iwo Jima.

On this date, 40 years ago, it was too late . . . again.

SAM ERVIN DIES

23 April 1985

As you can imagine, immediately following Sam Ervin's death, our newsroom became flooded with background information on him from every conceivable source, and I read most of it.

The first thing that struck me was the way he rushed through Harvard Law School so he could get a job and afford to marry his wife, who, he said later, he feared would marry someone else if he didn't get a move on.

This "Old Country Lawyer," as he often called himself, was obviously a screaming romantic. And if his life provided a clue to anything else he loved more than his bride, it was the United States Constitution.

He believed it to be the finest document ever created by the human mind. In the days when he fought against human rights issues and the E.R.A., it was because he thought the Constitution already covered it all, and that any *additional* law that didn't benefit every American *equally,* as the Constitution does, was a bad law. The Great Romantic lost.

The man who swore Samuel J. Erwin into office as a U.S. Senator for the first time, in the summer of 1954, was Vice President Richard M. Nixon. They would part company forever in May of 1973 when President Nixon would insult and flaunt the document he, too, had swore to protect and defend. And this time, the Great Romantic won.

I don't know about you, but I'm gonna miss that old man.

APARTHEID

26 April 1985

Why don't we begin with what might be called the *practical* American viewpoint—the one that says no matter what we do, let's don't do it *fast* because South Africa is in the Western Block and therefore an ally. Not to forget its historical link to Great Britain or that it supplies the Western World with massive amounts of raw materials we can get almost nowhere else, such as metals ranging from platinum to chromium to cadmium, all and more of which American investments are heavily married to, including a good number of South African branches of several American firms.

Then there's the item called "Sullivan Principles" named after an American clergyman, which asks that American firms over there not discriminate against blacks in any way, shape or form. Some adhere to these principles, some do not, but since American businesses employ such a tiny part of the South African work force, it's a "spit in the ocean" at best.

The *unpractical* American viewpoint? I don't care about *any* of that. Second class citizenship insults the soul of an American and we cannot support apartheid on purpose or by economic accident.

And the *last* unpractical argument? Americans are not the enemies of South Africans, white or black. We wish them both well because they are irrevocably tied to each other. It's their land, their home, and the only future they have will be the one they share together. They have absolutely no choice, as it is here in America.

The *unpractical* Americans who are banding together in protest across this land are trying to warn the South African government: You're out of time *now,* and you can forget about business as usual. Come here, please, and we will show you our graves, the ones marked *Civil War,* the ones marked *Watts.*

ANNIVERSARY OF THE FALL OF SAIGON

30 April 1985

This is a difficult essay for me to do because I lived in Saigon for the better part of a year under the auspices of "Uncle Sugar" and "The Army" in 19 and 70. I was 20 years old then, and a lot of pictures come to mind at the mention of that city's old name. My mother at the airport in Seattle sending me off to war, is one of those pictures. Though she teared up, she didn't cry out loud. I was very proud of her. I'm her only son.

The plane flight from Travis Air Force Base to Hawaii to Wake Island to Japan to Ben Hoa Air Base just north of Saigon and the bus trip into Saigon, are well remembered.

For my part, I entertained the troops. I worked for Special Services in Saigon and did a lot of performing all over the country as an actor and comic. There was a rumor that because entertainers were a "morale factor," the North Vietnamese had a price on our heads, which, if so, they nearly collected a couple of times.

War is never what you expect. They can teach you how to shoot straight, and you always did know how to run as fast as you can, but beyond that, it's a vicious shotgun blast of life and death. In short, I'm still confused.

A soldier, even the least of them, is not the one to ask about the *end* of the war. No matter which war, which side, we've only got two things to tell you. We're glad we lived through it, most of the time, and we're glad it's over.

MEMORIAL DAY

27 May 1985

I remember when I was in Vietnam and had occasion to travel out into what was considered hostile territory to entertain the troops. I would only then get a good look at the guys who stood between me in Saigon and those who would do me harm in the North. And as soon as those guys left, Saigon and everything else in the South fell.

But I've never forgotten their faces, the ones in the infantry, the ones closest to death.

One's first observation is the obvious fact that the vast majority of them are boys, many without beards yet, which presumably is the same for all wars, all sides. Eventually though, you start seeing things which leave no doubt in your mind but that these are really *old* men, old men who are ill.

Their eyelids, fingers, hands, arms twitch. And their eyes are always moving, looking. They go silent in the middle of a conversation because words mean nothing to them anymore, only sounds. At every opportunity, they get so drunk or stoned they throw-up straight in the air, and yet, in the midst of that, can become sober in a *click*. Vicious killers who cry and who get chills in 125 degree heat. Very *very* ill.

And today is Memorial Day . . . when we say, we think, we miss, we cry . . . for those once among us, who ran out of time, who fell down ill just short of the cure: Home.

FATHER'S DAY

16 June 1985

My dad, as I understand it, would fall under the general heading of a "40's Man." That is, he didn't kiss or hug kids, never said "I love you" to them and didn't have a whole lot to say or do with them unless they were in some kind of trouble.

I was an only child, my folks divorced when I was about twelve and I've never seen nor heard from my father since.

So when the time came for me to marry and have children, I was going to be different: In the delivery room, change the diapers, help feed 'em, tickle toes and knees, hug and kiss 'em constantly, break up fights, and say I love them out loud and often. Which I did.

Then came *my* divorce. Divorce court leaves you with about eleven cents. And with the geographical distance now between them and me, I've essentially become just like my dad.

What's the point? Enjoy them while you can, dads. One way or another, you're running out of time.

And all things considered, I think I miss most being touched. I got used to that.

ROCK HUDSON CONTRACTS AIDS

23 July 1985

I guess we're going to hear a lot of things about Rock Hudson in the next few days since he's obviously dying. And one of those things that will be discussed is whether or not he's gay. Such speculation will have something to do with the fact that the French hospital he's now in is famous for the treatment of AIDS. An issue, I think I can say without fear of contradiction, that won't amount to much, one way or another, here in the Bay Area. Which makes this just one more day I'm glad I'm a San Francisco kid and wasn't raised somewhere else.

The rest of the country can go crackers over the issue of Rock Hudson's sexual preference but few of us here, I suspect, will have the inclination or the time. There's too much fresh air coming off the Pacific, too much beauty in our communities to not off-set the human tragedies, too much communication between different lifestyles to let blind bigotry go unquestioned—and confusion last forever.

We're lucky: We can actually afford to think only of Rock Hudson as a human being, or an actor who gave us roaring laughter in the likes of *Pillow Talk,* the pain that comes with *A Farewell to Arms,* and made us bristle with pride during his valiant battle with "Sarge" in the diner in *Giant,* and all for that Mexican-American grandson.

Sleep well, Roy Scherer, Junior.

HIROSHIMA ANNIVERSARY

6 August 1985

We Americans like to think we have an enormous heart, that we bleed as hard as any nation when we are cut, that our mothers and fathers weep from the depths of their souls, too, when their children die in war. It is pain of that magnitude which proves there is no difference between America, Great Britain, Japan, Germany, Russia, China or any nation you can name who supplied the blood stream for World War II.

We are sorry for the bombs that took the lives of innocents at Hiroshima and Nagasaki. And we are the first to admit it must not happen again, ever.

Japan's Prime Minister, however, on this occasion, speaking perhaps more to the Japanese than to the world, called the bombings, and I quote, "An inhuman act" and an "indiscriminatory attack" on civilians which, therefore, he notes, was a "breach of international law."

We don't have to take that, Mr. Nakasone. As an elected leader of your people, you have the right to lecture Americans on any number of topics, but barbarism isn't one of them. Not after Pearl Harbor, you don't, and as for the slaughter of innocents, look to what your forces did in China, Korea, the Phillipines and *anywhere* they occupied, for that matter.

From the late 1930's to 1945 you marched straight into hell with the rest of us. And lest you forget it, Japan and Germany lead the way. You got worse than you dished out, you sowed what you reaped, millions died and we don't sleep . . . like we used to.

It was a barberous thing we did to Japan. Your statement is not wrong, Mr. Nakasone, just too late . . . and about an old fight. There's a new and more important fight, the last one, and we need each other now.

DAN WHITE KILLS HIMSELF

21 October 1985

Dan White is dead, and if the reports of his suicide by asphyxiation in a garage at his Excelsior District home in San Francisco are proven to be true, then what Dan White did on November 27, 1978, as the ancients used to say, has "had its way" with him.

Not in the history of this city, during the memory of most of us alive today anyway, will we ever have a better example of what simple violence does to sophisticated lives. I agree wholeheartedly with Mayor Feinstein: The Dan White book should be closed and his wife and children left alone to rebuild their lives and, maybe someday, forget most of it.

Since his release from prison on January 6th of last year, Dan White kept an extremely low profile, grew a beard, changed the color of his hair, made every effort apparently to maintain a family life and even tried to rekindle old friendships in San Francisco, but nothing worked, nothing could save his life.

Perhaps waiting to *be* killed, he killed himself. Perhaps suspecting justice had not been done, he administered it himself. Though more than likely, it was the knowledge that no man can function as an island, and since he was, he may have embraced the "friend" that death is sometimes rumored to be.

WELLES AND BRYNNER DIE

10 October 1985

Few would dispute, I imagine, that with the death of Orson Wells, the entertainment world has lost one of its few bona fide geniuses. And I define an entertainment genius as one who not only contributes his or her talents, but one who leads the industry and, in fact, is so innovative and imaginative that the industry will never be the same, and better for it.

Whether it be *The War of the Worlds* on radio in 1933, which gave us a taste of the frightening potential of mass communications, or the movie Welles wrote, directed and starred in, *Citizen Kane,* in 1944, which broke new cinemagraphic ground on a dozen levels, he easily qualifies as a genius, though due mostly to work done in his youth.

With the exception of that unique and ominous voice, which he would periodically lend to one small project or another, the last half of his professional life paled by comparison. Orson Wells is gone like few will go with none but the slightest chance his caliber will be seen again.

As for the death of Yul Brynner . . . well, we Americans are funny about royalty: We *elect* our *kings* here, and they are good. So when we say "The King is dead" we accordingly become the subjects . . . of much sadness.

VETERAN'S DAY

11 November 1985

There are so many things said about American veterans on this day and hardly anyone hears them. We've got better things to do, lives to live.

Today I poured through a pile of stories about parades few attended, speeches, shots fired into the air where shots belong, if they belong anywhere.

I'd like to share with you just one phrase that reached out to me from all the stuff I read. It was spoken by a Vietnam veteran at the Alamo in San Antonio, after a 300 mile march with other veterans from Dallas. The phrase was, "There's a patrol still out."

"There's a patrol still out." Obviously, a reference to soldiers still unaccounted for in Southeast Asia. But we never do get them all back, do we? Not even the ones who live through it and so many of the ones who don't.

It's peculiar, don't you think, when a war is over, to *not* be able to rest until those who can no longer come home are *brought* home?

And if only for taps, the sound of hammers—on nails.

THANKSGIVING

28 November 1985

I was interviewing some children for a feature story years ago in Detroit, I believe, and at one point, in reference to what they thought America meant, one of the children said, "America means everybody."

And that line has kind of haunted me over the years, especially when it comes to American immigrants like the original Pilgrims in 1607. They were certainly the most famous immigrants to sit themselves down and give formal *thanks* for some of the blessings we may assume are uniquely American.

But if America really *is* everybody, if the child was right, as they can sometimes be in a startling fashion, then we, I think, should be *thankful* for that fact and not intimidated by it.

Yet are we not intimidated *now* by the arrival of too many Central Americans? Proceeded by our fear of too many Vietnamese, or Taiwanese, Philippine or Mexican immigrants, and before that the Cubans and back through history, Asians, blacks, the Irish and virtually every race, creed, color and nationality that the child referred to as "everybody?" And these immigrants never went home, did they?

America became their home and though they may call their children by the names of their grandparents in keeping with their heritage, they want them to *think* like Americans: That girl children are as valuable as boys, that American democracy is not freedom, but the *demanding* of freedom, that we are all different and yet the same and therefore, if America is to go forward, we either go together, every last one of us, or the trip's in vain, and America is no more.

If we all made one step in that direction this year, I'm thankful.

CHRISTMAS

25 December 1985

This day of course is really a religious holiday, a Christian one to be specific, during which Christians commemorate the birth of Christ. I was raised in that general direction, though as the years went by I realized there are many different religions, Christian and otherwise.

Then I began to wonder which religion was the right one, and asking didn't help because all the various believers said their religion was and that everybody else's was wrong. The answer I think I settled for was that one's religion seems to be based on how you are raised, which religion your family practiced. Then, generally speaking, if your family is very religious, you will tend to be, and if not, you won't care much either.

But that answer didn't do for long because I found the biggest difference in life was not so much *religion,* but what that religion *accomplished* in terms of producing good people, ones who don't purposely harm others.

I found out eventually that there are a lot of bad people in this world and many of them claim to be very religious. They cheat on their spouses, steal and lie constantly, and the only time they ever genuinely care is if and when they are caught.

And if they are never caught, they smile and celebrate the religious holidays with the same gusto as those who have a conscience, which is one of the greatest services any religion will ever supply.

YEVTUSHENKO: "WARNOGRAPHY"

5 January 1986

I have been known to slap a couple of sentences together and call it a poem, so I've heard of Yevgeny Yevtushenko, though I must admit I'm not what you'd call a fan of his. I find his work a bit like the borscht of his country; thin and hard. Yet more than once he has produced poetic observations that are unnerving.

He also seems to have a particularly rare quality about him, one he had before he became famous, that being a strong sense of what I call "common truth," an attribute I suspect the Soviet government somehow got itself backed into tolerating because common or obvious truths make people, even governments, look painfully stupid when ignored.

Well, Yevtushenko was at an international press conference the other day in Moscow, with a gaggle of Soviet cultural leaders. The poet offered his opinion on the rise in the West of films like *Rambo, Red Dawn* and *Rocky IV,* the latter involving a Soviet boxer who becomes a target of American pride.

Yevtushenko called these kinds of films promoting nationalism and *justifiable* violent conflict "Warnography," as in the sexy, graphic selling of war.

Now, is that just a typical or expected comment from a Russian accusing American business or government of the mass hypnosis of its population?

I think not. The best of poets never climb on trains going nowhere. They either drag their feet, or try to lead. Yevtushenko does both today, giving us a new word; "Warnography."

NOT HERS, BUT MY DIVORCE CLASS!

10 January 1986

Ya know what? I'm not going to talk about the lady lawyer in Escondido who feels it's her ethical responsibility to teach you all about divorces. *I'm* going to do it once and only once, so buckle up!

There are two kinds of thieves in this country: Criminals and some divorce lawyers. And between the two, considering the odds, you've got a lot more to fear from the lawyers.

If you are the only one working when you divorce, your soon-to-be ex-spouse's lawyer will set an hourly fee from high to outrageous and there's absolutely nothing you can do about it. If you divorce and *both* are working, *each* will get robbed blind for no other reason than the lion's share of the one house you probably own together will have to be sold to cover legal fees.

With the courts backed up as they are, it can take as long as three years to finalize a divorce, which gives both lawyers a field day for filing and counter-filing papers, all of which you'll pay for by the *minute.*

But that aside, the most important thing to remember is your lawyer is nothing *vaguely* resembling a friend. They are in it 99 and 44 one-hundreths percent for the money. Both lawyers will call you names behind your back and the only lawyer who cares even less than your lawyer is the judge, who, you can bet your life, above all else, will make sure your lawyers get paid because that's how divorces work. If you think you got raped in the marriage, just wait until the professionals are done with you in court!

I'm mad as hell, and I'm not going to take anymore!

THE FIRST MARTIN LUTHER KING JR. NATIONAL HOLIDAY OBSERVANCE EVER

20 January 1986

I don't know about you, but I can't say I've ever spent much time wondering about what future Americans will think of you and me when we're gone. I guess I've been guilty of worrying about my own life and times and turmoils and just figured I'll let future Americans worry about themselves.

But some of us apparently do most definitely live for the future. In our lifetime, Dr. Martin Luther King Jr. was surely one who did. I guess proof that he belonged best to the future was that he was barely welcome in his own time and would be considered a hero by the vast majority of us only later.

We look back on his efforts now, and the efforts of others he has come to represent, and we say, "Sure, of course. Why *not* racial equality?" and now-a-days treat it as little more than one of our famous self-evident truths which—may he rest in peace—it has become.

But from all I've ever read about the man and heard from those who knew him, I doubt he would have approved of all this hoopla over his personal accomplishments. And mainly because his future, where he preferred to live, *dreamed* to live, has yet to arrive.

I suspect if he were with us now, even more than objecting to his being labeled an American hero, he would warn us in his eloquent and mind-boggling manner that the struggle to bring racial equality to this nation and the world is still in its infancy, and that this last most delicate child will die if we cannot find a way, all of us, each in our turn, to breathe life into its lungs until it can breathe on its own and say its first words: "I *am* the dream!"

GEORGE WASHINGTON'S BIRTHDAY

17 February 1986

Let's see, for the record, George Washington was born February 22, 1732, in Westmoreland County, Virginia, the 22nd being next Saturday, of course, though we celebrate his birth on the third Monday in February, which is today, according to U.S. Public Law 90-363. Whew!

Washington died December 14, 1799, at age 67. The first general of our army and the first president of our nation, he was called in his own lifetime, "First in war, first in peace and first in the hearts of his countrymen."

There is no way now-a-days, I feel, to recount the accomplishments of George Washington without eventually saying, "Come on, name me a nation that doesn't deify its first leader, ultimately producing more fantasy than fact?"

So I won't do that if you don't mind, but rather, remind you of something you know yourself and something you can believe: There is no one the British would have liked to see *dead* more than Washington. Of all our revolutionary leaders, no one's family had more to fear than his, and, if America had lost its war for independence, the chance of his continued existence, and that of his family, on their land, in their home with its possessions, would have been a gruesome impossibility.

Let us, perhaps, remember he did what needed to be done at the time, and once Americans began the struggle, those who did so never looked back but only ahead to that faint smile you and I now have on our faces.

REAGAN CALLS FOR MARCOS TO RESIGN
24 February 1986

There are some nations, we may assume, that America will always have a special relationship with and the Philippines is one of them. As the saying goes out West, we and the Philippine people "have been to the well together," a reference to the time when, if you wanted to go down to the river for a bucket of water, you took your life in your hands and, if you had one, you took a good friend with you for protection.

World War II was the "well," and you can ask almost any American who fought in or around the Philippines, they went "back and forth" with us every time. It must never be forgotten that this special relationship has exacted a ghastly price historically and the Filippinos paid it with us, life for life, when they could have chosen differently.

Therefore, it has to be extremely difficult for President Reagan to call for Marcos' resignation, regardless of the situation, adding the fact that democracies, even in turmoil, don't like to be dictated to from the outside.

We can't just go in and toss Marcos out. We can't go in there and *do* anything, in fact. It's not like they're under attack from a foreign army. And what will happen if the U.S. cuts aid to the Philippines? Who will that hurt? The Marcos household? We doubt it somehow.

No. It has to be done by the Philippine people. And we will wait, outside their house, as friends do, until the illness passes, and celebrate with them when they recover.

MYRON COHEN DIES

11 March 1986

There's something particularly difficult in saying good-bye to a comic if you happen to think of yourself as one, also. I don't know why that is but I know what it feels like. If everybody calls you funny all your life and then someone you always thought was funny dies, it means that something that keeps you alive, now no longer keeps that other comic alive.

And it's not a simple fear of death either. It's the realization that the only thing you were ever any good at will leave you someday, and that being funny, such as it is, was all you ever really had.

I first saw Myron Cohen on *The Ed Sullivan Show* years ago and would see him "live" in New York City twice. Each and every time, live anyway, I laughed until I cried. He was so funny you couldn't believe it, and if you never saw him work, let me tell you how rare he was.

With his oft-used Yiddish accent, he was one of those rare comics who could make you laugh so long and so hard, you actually began to fear for your health.

He was a former salesman in Manhattan's garment district and later one of the best known "Borscht Belt" story tellers in New York's famous Catskill mountains . . . and now dead in Nyak, wouldn'tcha know?

Goodbye, Mister Cohen. Save me a seat in the back?

THE END

INDEX

ABOUT THE AUTHOR

Wayne Shannon was born in Spokane, Washington, on January 16, 1948. His parents moved to the San Francisco Bay area soon thereafter where Wayne remained until age 12. (see CHINESE NEW YEAR, page 31)

After the family returned to the state of Washington, Wayne attended junior high and high school in the small community of Moses Lake. Following high school, he went to the American Academy of Dramatic Art in New York City, appeared off-Broadway as an actor and directed children's theater off-*off*-Broadway.

Back in Washington, he graduated from Highline Community College in Midway, near Seattle.

Shannon served in Special Services of the U.S. Army and went to both Vietnam (see ANNIVERSARY OF THE FALL OF SAIGON, page 105, and MEMORIAL DAY, page 106) and Germany. Following his time in the service, he returned to Seattle and graduated from the University of Washington.

Earlier, during his junior high and junior college days, he performed as an amateur/professional comedian, which laid the foundation for his later work.

He began his television career in the Seattle area and this led to employment in Detroit (see THE NIGHT THE LIGHTS WENT OUT ON NADER, page 47) and Philadelphia. He currently appears on KRON-TV Channel 4 in San Francisco, the city Wayne always considered home.

He has been married twice and divorced once (see NOT HERS, BUT *MY* DIVORCE CLASS pg 116). There were children.

MAY-MURDOCK PUBLICATIONS
Drawer 1346 - 90 Glenwood Avenue
Ross CA 94957 - (415) 454-1771

RAILROAD BOOKS BY DICK MURDOCK

SMOKE IN THE CANYON: My Steam Days in Dunsmuir
144 pages, 63 historical photographs,   hard cover $25.95
original artwork by Charles Endom   perfect bound 15.95

PORT COSTA 1879-1941: A Saga of Sails, Sacks and Rails
40 pages, historical photographs,
original artwork by Charles Endom   saddle stitched 6.00

HOGHEADS & HIGHBALLS: Railroad Lore and Humor
64 pages, sketches by Charles Endom   perfect bound 5.00

LOVE AFFAIR WITH STEAM
40 pages,   saddle stitched 3.00

EARLY CALL FOR THE PERISHABLES: A Day at the Throttle
24 pages   saddle stitched 2.00

WALNUT CREEK'S UNIQUE OLD STATION
24 pages 17 photographs,   saddle stitched 2.00

BOOKS BY JAYNE MURDOCK

I PAINTED ON A BRIGHT RED MOUTH: The War Years,
Dec. 1941-Aug. 1945
64 pages, vintage photo-collages   perfect bound 6.00

UNTIL DEATH AND AFTER; How to Live With a Dying Intimate
64 pages   perfect bound 5.00

BRIEF INFINITY: A Love Story in Haiku
64 pages   perfect bound 5.00

LOVE LINES: A True Love Story in Lyric Prose
by Jayne May & Dick Murdock, 134 pages   perfect bound 5.00

Send for free brochure
MONEY BACK GUARANTEE ON ALL
MAY-MURDOCK PUBLICATIONS

COLOPHON

Typesetting: QuadraType, 2201 Third Street, San Francisco, 94107 using Quadex Q5000 Equipment and the Kurzweil System 4000 Scanner
Type: Garamond Book
Paper: 60# white smooth offset
Cover photograph: Michael Pechner
Color separation: Product Agency Inc., 125 Larkspur, San Rafael, California, 94901
Design & Layout: Jayne Murdock
Printing and Binding: Spilman Printing, 1801 9th Street, Sacramento, California, 95894

ORDER FORM

MAY-MURDOCK PUBLICATIONS
DRAWER 1346
Ross CA 94957

Please send me _____ copies of SHANNON: What's it all mean? @$5.95 each.

Name _____

Address _____

City _____ State _____ Zip _____

CALIFORNIA residents please add 36¢ sales tax per book.
SHIPPING: $1.00 for first book, 50¢ each additional book.